FRENCH FLAMBÉ COOKING

AT HOME

DAVID & KATHY JORDAN

FRENCH FLAMBÉ COOKING
AT HOME

Step by step recipes and guidance to flambé delicacies for family and friends

PHOTOGRAPHY AND FOOD STYLING
BY MICHELLE SHIPLEY

*To my identical twin, Darrell, who was my partner in crime
and to my wife, Kathy, my partner in life and cooking*

Acknowledgements

I am so appreciative to those who trained me in the Art of French Tableside Service and the Art of Flambéing. From the Eugene Hotel, John Anderson, General Manager, took a chance to hire identical twin 17-year-old teenage boys, and Ib Hamide, my Flame Captain, taught me how to set up a service cart, recipes, and how to prepare and present tableside. From the Rodeway Inn, Walide Saleeby, my Maitre d', I learned the flair and finesse and how to enhance the drama of the presentation. Walide taught me that being a Flambé Chef was to be an artist and a showman.

My customers had the greatest influence. I enjoyed watching them watching me prepare the item they had ordered. Their eyes glistened with joy and I loved hearing their oooo's and ahhhh's. To my customers a huge, heartfelt thank you for your enthusiastic response.

My friends and family have been delighted over the years by my preparing tableside delicacies. They request their favorites which allows me to remember the recipes and to practice the art in the use of the French fork and spoon service. To my friends and family, I appreciate your love of the Art of Flambé.

My wife Kathy is my consummate sous chef. She helped me with every aspect in the development of this cookbook from preparing ingredients to food stylist to creating recipes. I love working with her side by side in our kitchen.

Contents

Acknowledgements   i

A thank you to those individuals who contributed meaningful support.

Foreword   1

Learn more about Chef David, namely, his history, experiences, and repertoire of knowledge.

Introduction   4

Learn about the art and history of French Flambé cooking. Explore the rich tradition and craft behind the flame.

Set the Stage   5

This will give you all the practical introductory information that you need to know before you light the flame - what equipment to use, helpful Tips from the Flambé Chef, and a Step by Step to get you familiarized with the art of flambéing.

Act I ~ Starters   20

With everything from Cranberries and Sizzling Brie to Steak Tartare, this section completely covers appetizers.

Act II ~ Entrées   37

The entrées in this section are to die for, with recipes ranging from Steak Au Poivre to Crab Legs Voltaire.

Act III ~ Desserts   101

Who in their right mind wouldn't finish off the night without a sweet treat? This section mixes sugar with flame to produce delicacies from Bananas Foster to Cherries Jubilee.

Encore   144

Of course, a meal is also never complete without a drink. This section includes recipes for Café Brûlot Diabolique, Spanish Coffee, and more.

Supporting Cast   155

These recipes are the "supporting cast" of the acts. They support other dishes that simply would not be the same without them.

Index   195

Got questions? Lost something? Look no further.

Foreword

When I was 17 and a junior at Pleasant Hill High School, in Pleasant Hill, Oregon, I began exploring careers. I became interested in hotel management and wanted to attend Cornell University. To attend Cornell, I needed to be sponsored by a 5-star hotel. My high school counselor referred me to the Eugene Hotel, located in Eugene, Oregon, and set up an interview appointment with the General Manager.

At the time I didn't have my driver's license, so I asked Darrell, my identical twin brother, to drive me to my interview appointment. I met with John Anderson, General Manager, to discuss my interest in hotel management and John asked that I come back in the summer if I wanted a job. Summer arrived and I wanted a job. So, I called and set up another interview appointment. Darrell again drove me to my interview and, also, went to my interview. Not only did I get offered a position, John offered Darrell a position too.

In the summer of 1972, Darrell and I started an apprenticeship where we were instructed on wines, food and wine pairings, cooking, polite conversation, flambé food preparation and presentation and the Art of French Tableside Service. Yes folks, two 17-year-olds were recommending wines and handling and serving alcohol. Oops, in Oregon minors handling alcohol was against the law — no problem there!! In fact, an Oregon Liquor Control Commission Agent visited the Eugene Hotel one evening and saw Darrell and he asked Darrell, "how old are you?" to which Darrell responded, "let me get the Maitre d'". We never asked any questions but after the Agent met with the Maitre d' that evening we never saw him again.

Being a French Flambé Chef at an early age was fun and very unique. First, I don't know many 17-year-olds who go to work in a full tuxedo! While my fellow classmates were doing entry level jobs, Darrell and I were doing something that was somewhat glamorous in a five-star dining room.

Because Darrell and I were handling alcohol people assumed we were 21-year-old adults and had that level of maturity. When in reality we were 17- to 18-year-old adults just starting to have a reasonable level of maturity and starting to date.

The novelty of having "twins" preparing your meal tableside was the talk of Eugene and Springfield. Our flambé preparations were fun to watch and delicious. Our "small incidents", such as catching a tablecloth on fire in a packed dining room, were so memorable that our customers would return for another exciting evening and meal!

This cookbook is about preserving recipes I learned to prepare at the Eugene Hotel and the Rodeway Inn and sharing these recipes for others to enjoy. It is also in memory of my brother, Darrell, as he walked down this path with me into our future careers in the restaurant industry.

French tableside service tips and the steps to flambé are featured in the cookbook. The recipes are a trip down memory lane into the 1960's and 1970's when tableside service was the standard and the definition of elegance at a fine dining restaurant.

The recipes that follow are rich, decadent, and loaded with calories...did I say loaded with calories?! Some recipes are relatively easy while others need some pre-preparation. Bottom- line is that the time and effort to make these recipes are well worth it. If serving one or more recipes at a dinner party, your guest will think they have died and gone to food heaven.

The recipes in this cookbook are flambé recipes I learned as a Flambé Chef at the Eugene Hotel and Rodeway Inn, French classics, popular recipes, and new recipes that my wife, Kathy, and I created.

Enjoy and Bon Appetit!

Identical Twins
Darrell Jordan and David Jordan Flambé Chefs
1974

Introduction

In the late 19th century, cooks were not seen or heard from in a restaurant, Georges Auguste Escoffier changed all that. He stepped out of the back of the house and into the front of the house and the world changed. He engaged his customers, found out what their tastes were, what they liked and what they didn't like. He then kept copious notes on them, which allowed him to make the perfect dinner for them when they came to his restaurant.

Along with his notes, Chef Escoffier liked to name recipes after some of his more famous guests. Several reasons come to mind for him doing this. One, no greater tribute to ones' self than seeing your name next to a dish in a fancy eating establishment, the ultimate vanity project! Two, it let diners identify and perhaps become, for a little while, that celebrity when they ordered that particular meal. Three, it gave the great chef something to talk about especially if the guest was a woman, as the great chef was a lover of women.

Just what is French Tableside Service anyways? It is an elegant style of restaurant service that the French Chef Escoffier originated in the late 1800's. In this style of service, the waiter or French Flambé Chef comes to the dining table and prepares and serves an appetizer, salad, entrée or dessert in front of the guest. For more flair and drama, food might be flambéed. Flambé, the French word for flame, is liquor poured over the food and ignited leaving the subtle flavor of the alcohol to complement the dish being prepared.

In the following pages I have given you the history of the recipe, if it is known, tasting notes and flavor descriptions, personal stories, and tips about the dish. Hopefully the recipe introductions will allow you to get to know the chef who is credited with originating flambé cooking, Chef Escoffier, who is also known as the "Chef of Kings and the King of Chefs."

French Tableside Service is all about the show and selling the "sizzle." Customers and guests alike are mesmerized by the flair and style of preparing or flambéing food at the table.

It's SHOWTIME!

4

Set The Stage

French Tableside Service Equipment

Having the right equipment for service and flambéing is all part of the show and French presentation.

The following are the basics of French Tableside and Flambéing equipment that I use during preparations:

Rechaud is the French word for stove or burner. Rechaud's can use spirits, ethanol, butane, or propane for a flame to heat a skillet, saucepan or chafing dish. My preferred rechaud is the portable butane stove by Iwatani. It is light weight, perfect size for up to a 12-inch skillet, and easy to clean.

If you don't have a rechaud and don't have the equipment to work by your dining table, your cooktop or your burners of your stovetop will work just as well. I find that my company, with glass of wine in hand, will join me in the kitchen when I'm preparing a recipe on my cooktop.

Chafing Dish is a deep pan with a handle set in a stand with an alcohol burner. A Chafing Dish allows for easier handling of a sauce to be mixed, such as Crab Legs Voltaire, and can be more visually appealing such as when preparing the flaming coffee Café Brûlot Diabolique.

Gueridon is a small ornamental, moveable table that is set-up tableside for either preparation of a salad, carving of meat, filleting of seafood, or preparing flambé dishes. For my gueridon table at home, I use my wife's hostess cart that rolls and has fold out leaves that I can open to accommodate the portable stove, equipment and food. It also has a bottom shelf that I can put used dishes out of the way.

If using a fine hostess cart, to protect the cart, be sure to use a pad under the table linen. When preparing items, fat will pop and splatter and soak into a table linen.

Stainless Steel Lined Skillet in a 10-inch to 12-inch size is ideal for preparing most recipes. My personal favorite long handled skillets are by Mauviel and Spring Culinox, both are made with brass and copper and lined in stainless steel. You can find Mauviel at kitchen stores such as Williams-Sonoma and directly through Spring Culinox or can be found on eBay®.

These pans heat up quickly with even heat distribution. Please note,

Non-stick skillets are not designed for high-intensity cooking and should not be used for flambéing.

Large Serving Fork and Spoon included in flatware sets are perfect for cooking and stirring the ingredients in the skillet. They are also long enough to avoid the flames when flambéing a recipe.

Butter Warmer is ideal to gently warm the alcohol to be flambéed. The Norpro Ceramic Butter Warmer is a small ceramic saucepan heated over a candle and is a great option.

Long Matches or Wand Lighter may be used to light the alcohol in the skillet. Wooden fireplace matches are longer, about 9 inches, and are made out of thicker, heavier wood to burn longer which gives you the time to light your dish without burning the fingers. Alternatively, a wand lighter, with the hold down trigger, works perfectly without worrying if it will go out or burn your fingers.

Irish Coffee Mugs by Libbey are the perfect glass for a Spanish, Irish, or Café Royal coffees. The footed 8-ounce mug is designed to showcase a coffee drink and is made of thick glass for strength and maintaining the coffee's heat.

Decorative Dishes for presentation of the ingredients for the recipe. My wife likes to shop garage sales for unusual bowls and plates.

Hot Pad to hold onto the skillet when the handle is warm. There are silicone hot handle holders that fit onto the skillet handle.

Damp Towel is essential for cleaning drops and splatters from the edges of the plate or bowl.

Spoon Rest for the fork and spoon.

BACARDÍ
SUPERIOR
DRY SACK
Grand Marnier
MALIBU
BUSHMILLS
BLACK BUSH
MYERS'S
RUM
KUYPER

Tips from the Flambé Chef

The following are my tips to successful French tableside service and flambé.

Since it is all about the show, it is essential to prepare and set-up your "stage", and, if need be, rehearse your recipe until you have confidence in your presentation skills.

- Set a gueridon, hostess cart, bar cart, or card table next to the dining table or in the presentation area; cover with a table linen or set-up a kitchen counter or bar.

- Set up and organize cart, tabletop or counter with the equipment needed for the recipe to be prepared and served.

- Flambé recipe equipment will include, but not be limited to, a rechaud known as a portable gas burner, stainless steel skillet, a long-handled wand lighter or long match, large spoon and fork, spoon rest, hot pads, and damp towel.

- Organize and set-up serving dishes in presentation area.

- For recipes served cold, chill salad plates and forks and pre-scoop and freeze ice cream in bowls or on a tray or platter.

- For recipes served warm, warm plates or platters in oven.

- Per recipe instructions, pre-prepare ingredients and dish-up the recipe ingredients in attractive dishes.

- Organize the ingredients on the cart or table in order of the preparation instructions and within arm's reach.

- Use avocado oil or avocado oil and butter together to sauté meats. Avocado oil has a higher smoke point and can handle the heat of the flambé. When oil is combined with butter in a recipe, it minimizes the risk of the butter burning and breaking from the sauce.

- For flambé recipes, use an 80-proof liquor or 40% alcohol by volume for flaming.

- When preparing entrées and desserts, use quality liquor, liqueurs, and wines to enhance and complement the flavors of the recipe. Using quality alcohol (these are the stars of the show), wine and liqueur can bring the wow factor to your preparations. I recommend for your pantry the following alcohols and liqueurs for the depth of flavor they add to a recipe:

Liqueurs	Liquor	Wine
99 Bananas	Don Q 151 Rum	Sandeman Founder's Reserve Ruby Porto
Cointreau	Bacardi White Rum	
DeKuyper Triple Sec	Blanton's Bourbon Whiskey or Woodford Reserve	Dry Sack Medium Sherry
Frangelico		Red and White Wines
Grand Marnier	Bushmills Black Bush Irish Whiskey	
Kahlua	Calvados Apple Brandy	
Malibu Caribbean Rum	Courvoisier VSOP Cognac	
Tia Maria	G.E. Massenez Pear Brandy	
	Meyers's Dark Rum	
	Schladerer Cherry Kirschwasser	

Remember, if an alcohol or wine tastes good enough to drink, then they are perfect for cooking.

- **Cold liquor will not ignite!** There are 2 methods you can use to heat and ignite the alcohol and flambé a recipe.

- *Safety first - As the flames can go quite high, for safety stand back a safe distance when lighting, tie long hair back, don't wear loose clothes or floppy sleeves, ensure plenty of clear height above the skillet for the flames, keep a lid nearby to cover the skillet in the event the flames are too large...and, just in case, a fire extinguisher close by.*

- The safest flambé method for a home cook is:

1) Put the alcohol into a small saucepan or butter warmer and gently warm the alcohol about 5 minutes to a temperature of 95 to 100°F,

2) Use a large spoon or fork to bring skillet ingredients back towards the skillet handle,

3) Pull the skillet back to heat the front of the skillet over the flame 1 to 2 seconds,

4) While the skillet front is over the flame, pour the warm liquor into front of the skillet, heat 1 to 2 seconds, and, standing back, use a long match or wand lighter to ignite the alcohol.

5) The fumes from the alcohol may ignite without the use of a long match or wand lighter.

- The method I use as a flambé chef is as follows,

1) Use a large spoon or fork to bring the skillet ingredients back towards the skillet handle,

2) Pull the skillet back to heat the front of the skillet over the flame 1 to 2 seconds,

3) While the skillet front is over the flame, pour the liquor into front of the skillet, heat 1 to 2 seconds,

4) Ignite the liquor by the rechaud flame igniting the alcohol fumes.

- Once the liquor is added to the skillet, do not delay lighting; otherwise, the food may absorb the raw alcohol and retain a harsh flavor.

- Cook until the flame starts to disappear as at this point the alcohol has burned off. Stir remaining alcohol into the sauce.

A Word of Caution:

Never pour liquor from a bottle into a skillet that has a flame or is near an open flame as the flame can follow the stream of alcohol into the bottle and cause it to explode!!

One of the cautionary tales related to me and my twin about exploding alcohol bottles was from our flame captain.

He was preparing a dessert when the flambé flames ignited a splash of alcohol from a bottle of 151 Rum and the flames followed the line of splash into the bottle which exploded. The explosion caught a customer's wig on fire, singed her eyelashes and eyebrows, and burned part of her dress and caught the dining room drapes on fire.

The story might have ended there in tragedy and a lawsuit, but these customers were very old customers of our flame captain. These customers came back the very next night and had the flame captain make the exact same meal to show their appreciation for his skills as a flambé chef.

Step by Step

Preparing Bourbon Whiskey Apple Flambé to illustrate the steps of flambéing:

1) Gueridon or Cart set-up for Flambé Service, food in decorative dishes and organized to the recipe.

2) Rechaud set on medium flame.

3) 12-inch skillet heated and adding butter.

4) Apples added to melted butter in skillet.

5) Sauté apples until softened but still firm.

6) Add brown sugar to apples, melt sugar.

7) Using the fork, pull apples back toward the skillet handle and pull skillet back to heat front. Add bourbon into front of skillet.

8) Heat 1 to 2 seconds, bourbon fumes will ignite from the flame of the rechaud or use a long match or wand lighter.

9) Carefully stir bourbon into apples and sauce.

10) Sprinkle ground cinnamon over apples and sauce.

11) Bring out ice cream from freezer and serve apples and sauce over ice cream.

12) A little sprinkle of ground cinnamon and Voile! Bourbon Whiskey Apple Flambé!!

Act I ~ Starters

Starters are the opening act for the evening. They are the tease that sets the theme and the hook which gets the guest's taste buds involved in the acts that are to follow.

Wilted Spinach Salad

Caeser Salad

Lollipop Lamb Chops with
Cherry Sauce

Steak Tartare

Cranberries and Sizzling Brie

Meatballs of Fire!

Scallops with Peach Chutney
Bourbon Sauce

Starters

Wilted Spinach Salad

Serves 2

Wilted Spinach is an old-fashioned dish, often considered German or Pennsylvania Dutch in origin. It consists of a hot dressing made quickly out of bacon grease, sugar, and vinegar. The Cognac adds a sweetness to balance with the saltiness of the bacon. Live dangerously and try something new.

Ingredients

4 cups fresh baby spinach, washed, dried, large stems removed

2 large eggs

4 slices bacon, cut in 1/2-inch pieces

2 tablespoons finely chopped red onion

1/2 cup red wine vinegar

1 tablespoon granulated sugar

1 ounce VSOP Cognac

Kosher salt and freshly ground black pepper to taste

Directions

Place spinach in a medium decorative salad bowl.

Place eggs in a saucepan large enough to hold them in a single layer. Add enough cold water to come at least 1-inch above the eggs. Heat over high heat to boiling. Turn off heat, remove from burner and cover pan with lid.

Let the eggs stand in the hot water about 12 minutes for large eggs. Immediately place eggs in ice water until they are completely cooled. Peel eggs, coarsely chop and place in an attractive bowl.

Place a 12-inch skillet on cooktop over medium heat, cook bacon until crispy; remove bacon and drain on paper towels. Leave bacon drippings in the skillet. Place bacon and the chopped red onion in attractive bowls.

Tableside Service:

Place the 12-inch skillet with the bacon drippings on a rechaud burner over medium flame heat. Add to the bacon drippings the red wine vinegar and sugar, heat to boiling to melt sugar, stirring to blend.

Pull skillet back to heat front of skillet, pour Cognac into front of skillet and heat front 1 to 2 seconds, light Cognac using a long match or long handled lighter, and immediately stir the Cognac into the dressing until flame goes out.

Add bacon into the dressing; pour dressing over spinach, toss gently. Place salad on serving plates and garnish with bacon bits, red onions and hard-boiled eggs.

Serve immediately.

Caeser Salad

Serves 2

Caesar Salad's creation is attributed to Caeser Cardini, an Italian chef and restaurant owner. He moved to Tijuana from California to avoid Prohibition, and it was here, on July 4th, 1924, that Caesar is believed to have invented the Caesar Salad. Cardini's recipe had six simple components -- full stalks of romaine, raw egg, olive oil, croutons, Parmesan cheese, and Worcestershire sauce.

Cardini developed the original Caeser Salad Dressing which did not contain anchovies. My recipe for Caeser salad dressing does include anchovies. My experience with anchovies is that most people haven't tried or tasted an anchovy and express a dislike for the tiny, salty fish. Anchovies are the salt in the dressing. I do find that when I make the dressing with anchovies, the response to the dressing is "yum!" and "delicious!" and surprise when they learn that it has anchovies.

I highly recommend you use some form of anchovy in this recipe, as it really needs the salt.

I have a number of friends who comment that I have ruined them when it comes to ordering a Caeser Salad in a restaurant – "it just doesn't taste as good as David's!". I feel that this is a testimonial to the use of anchovies in my dressing.

The secret to working with anchovies is that they need to be smashed to a paste to blend into the dressing. If you dislike bits of anchovy filet, anchovy paste is an excellent substitute as it blends easily into the dressing.

You may be wondering why I use coddled eggs in the recipe. Coddling an egg serves two purposes. Coddling partially cooks the egg white giving a creaminess to the salad dressing and it also minimizes the risk associated with salmonella.

*See "Supporting Cast" for Caeser Croutons recipe (page 159).

Ingredients

1 tablespoon garlic, coarsely chopped

1/4 cup extra-virgin olive oil

2 cups 200°F hot water

2 eggs

4 romaine leaves, washed, dried, cut into bite-sized pieces

2 teaspoons Worcestershire sauce

1/2 teaspoon dry mustard

1 teaspoon Dijon mustard

2 cloves garlic, minced or crushed

1/2 large juicy lemon or 1 whole lemon, cut in half

4 anchovy filets, finely chopped or 2 teaspoons anchovy paste

Kosher salt and freshly ground black pepper to taste

1/4 cup freshly shredded Parmesan cheese

1/2 cup Caeser Croutons*

4 whole anchovy fillets, *optional garnish*

Directions

In a small bowl, place chopped garlic in olive oil, let stand 1 hour then strain out garlic, pour into a decorative bowl. Place salad plates in freezer to chill.

Tableside Service:

Coddle eggs by using the spoon to gently place eggs into the hot water, leave eggs 4 to 5 minutes.

Spoon 1 tablespoon of garlic oil into a salad bowl; wipe the oil inside the bowl with your clean hand or a pastry brush. Place romaine leaves in salad bowl.

Break the coddled eggs into a medium bowl; add Worcestershire sauce, dry mustard, Dijon mustard, minced or crushed garlic, juice of the lemon half or halves, and chopped anchovies.

Using a fork, beat ingredients together; while beating, slowly drizzle in the remaining garlic oil. Season to taste with salt and pepper.

Pour dressing over the romaine. Sprinkle with Parmesan cheese and croutons to taste and toss salad together. Place salad on chilled plates, an optional garnish is to drape 2 anchovy fillets over the top of the salad.

Serve the salads with chilled forks.

Lollipop Lamb Chops with Cherry Sauce

Serves 2

I have listed this recipe in two areas in this cookbook because people forget where they saw it! This recipe can be an excellent starter or center of the plate super star, it is up to you. The Cherry Kirschwasser is a classy fruit forward "schnapps" that accentuates the cherry flavor of the cherries and cherry preserves.

Ingredients

1/4 cup dried cherries

1 ounce Schladerer Cherry Kirschwasser

3/4 cup water

2 tablespoons Minor's Demi Glace Sauce Concentrate

4 lollipop lamb chops from Frenched rack of lamb

Kosher salt and freshly ground black pepper

2 tablespoons avocado oil

1 large shallot, finely chopped

2 ounces Schladerer Cherry Kirschwasser

1 teaspoon Worcestershire sauce

1 teaspoon Dijon mustard

1/2 cup cherry preserves

1 tablespoon butter

Directions

Place cherries in a small microwaveable dish; pour 1 ounce Cherry Kirschwasser over the cherries. Microwave 30 seconds, set aside.

Place the 3/4 cup water in a microwaveable container and heat 1 minute in microwave; stir in the demi-glace concentrate. Pour demi-glace sauce into a pitcher.

To French a rack of lamb; first, place a knife blade about a quarter of an inch above the eye of the lamb chop and cut a line from the first rib to the other end of the rack. Now, run the knife blade between the ribs and cut down to the first cut line and then across to the next rib and up the rib forming a U pattern, now clean the rib of fat. Take the knife and cut the rib to make the chop.

Season lollipop lamb chops with salt and pepper.

Tableside Service:

Place a 12-inch skillet on a rechaud over medium flame heat; add avocado oil to skillet and heat until shimmering. Place lollipop lamb chops into the skillet and sear 3 to 4 minutes on both sides for rare, 120°F. Sauté longer for doneness as follows:

Medium-Rare - 125°F	Medium - 130°F
Medium-Well - 145°F	Well-Done - 150°F

Remove lamb chops from skillet and place on a warm plate. Add shallots to skillet and sauté until softened; add macerated cherries.

Using a spoon, pull sauce back towards skillet handle, pull skillet back to heat the front of the skillet, pour Cherry Kirschwasser into front of skillet and heat 1 to 2 seconds, using a long match or wand lighter ignite Kirschwasser.

Add demi-glace sauce, Worcestershire sauce, Dijon mustard, cherry preserves and stir. Simmer sauce until it reaches a sauce consistency.

Swirl in butter to finish sauce and serve sauce in a dunking bowl with the lamb chops.

Steak Tartare

Serves 2

There is interesting speculation as to how Steak Tartare came about. The most colorful tale is in the early 13th century Mongol riders placed slabs of horse meat under their saddles and ate the pulverized meat raw after a long day of soldiering. Another possibility is the dish evolved from the French Polynesian tradition of raw meat consumption. No matter how it came about, it's generally accepted that the original dish was made in the 1870 era with horse meat as beef was scarce.

Talk about a menu item making a comeback, I know...raw meat with spices? Like others, Kathy was reticent to try Steak Tartare, after all, a tenderloin steak should be grilled on the barbecue. For the record, when the finely chopped tenderloin is combined with the spices, topped on toasted French bread and garnished with Dijon mustard, capers, cornichons, parsley, and shallots, you will be surprised how the flavors meld together for a rich beef appetizer.

Ingredients

12 ounces beef tenderloin steak

1 lemon half

1 large egg

1/2 teaspoon dry mustard

1/4 teaspoon granulated garlic

1/4 teaspoon granulated onion

1/2 teaspoon kosher salt

1 teaspoon freshly ground black pepper

3 dashes Tabasco sauce

1 tablespoon Worcestershire sauce

1 1/2 tablespoons capers, drained

2 tablespoons Dijon mustard

1/4 cup minced shallot

1/2 ounce Dry Sack Medium Sherry

Garnish:

2 egg yolks

2 tablespoons drained capers

2 tablespoons minced cornichons

2 tablespoons finely chopped shallot

2 tablespoons Dijon mustard

2 tablespoons minced Italian parsley

4 slices toasted French baguette or Melba toast

Directions

Place steak in freezer, about 30 minutes, until the beef becomes crusted with ice crystals and is firm but not frozen. Remove steak from freezer, cut into 1/2-inch cubes, then chop the meat to a fine, coarse texture. Alternatively, divide the meat into 4 small batches and, using a food processor with steel blade, pulse each batch separately 3 to 4 pulses until meat is coarsely chopped but not finely ground. Place the chopped steak in an attractive medium bowl.

Prior to the tableside service carefully wash hands.

Tableside Service:

In the bowl with the chopped beef, using your tablespoon form a crater in the meat. In the center of the crater, break a whole egg. Add dry mustard, granulated garlic, granulated onion, salt and pepper, Tabasco sauce, Worcestershire sauce, capers, Dijon mustard, shallots, and sherry; gently mix together.

Using the spoon, portion meat onto 2 chilled plates molding into a round disc. Smooth the top and with the back of the tablespoon indent the meat to create a nest.

For presentation, place an egg yolk in the center indentation. Sprinkle minced parsley around edge of plate. Serve each plate with a garnish of 1 tablespoon each capers, cornichons, shallot, Dijon mustard, parsley, and toasted French baguette slices or Melba toast.

Cranberries & Sizzling Brie

Serves 4

The holiday season arrived and Kathy and I wanted to create a new holiday appetizer. We had our close friend Marie Arbios join us one afternoon as our official taste tester for the new appetizer. Baked Brie is always delicious with a topping of fruit; but, when the cranberry sauce with Christmas spices had a drizzle of flaming Grand Marnier and 151 Rum over the top, all Marie could say was "this is the best darned recipe I've had in years!"

Ingredients

3/4 cup granulated sugar

1/4 cup water

6 ounces fresh or frozen cranberries

1/4 teaspoon ground cinnamon

1/4 teaspoon ground allspice

1/8 teaspoon kosher salt

1/8 teaspoon ground ginger

1/8 teaspoon ground cloves

1 wheel (8 ounces) triple cream Brie

1/2 ounce Grand Marnier

1/2 ounce Don Q 151 Rum

Directions

Preheat oven to 350°F.

In a medium saucepan, combine sugar and water; bring to a boil. Add cranberries, cinnamon, allspice, salt, ginger, and cloves, reduce heat; simmer, uncovered, until berries pop and mixture is thickened, about 10 minutes. Place warm spiced cranberry sauce in a pitcher or gravy boat.

Unwrap brie, carefully slice off the top layer of rind to expose the brie and place in an 8-inch ovenproof dish. Bake 6 to 7 minutes until top of brie looks softened. Place dish on a service trivet.

Tableside Service:

In a small saucepan or butter warmer on a rechaud on low heat, warm Grand Marnier and 151 Rum.

Pour warm cranberry sauce to cover top of the brie. Using a long match or wand lighter, ignite the alcohol in the saucepan or warmer.

Start pouring a stream of flaming alcohol over the cranberry sauce and brie starting close to the brie and then rising for a dramatic effect of the flames.

Serve with sliced baguette, toasted or grilled if desired.

Meatballs of Fire!

Serves 4

A glass of wine, a few meatballs with a yogurt sauce to start your evening! This is the perfect appetizer to start a meal with and you will love the subtle flavor of the cinnamon in the meatballs.

*See "Supporting Cast" for the Yogurt Sauce recipe (page160).

Ingredients

1/2 pound ground pork

1/2 pound ground lamb

1/4 cup finely chopped red bell pepper

1/4 cup finely chopped onion

2 large cloves garlic, finely chopped

1/4 cup finely chopped cilantro

1/2 teaspoon ground cumin

1/8 teaspoon cayenne pepper

1/8 teaspoon ground cinnamon

1/8 teaspoon ground cloves

1/8 teaspoon ground cardamom

1/8 teaspoon freshly ground black pepper

1 teaspoon kosher salt

2 ounces VSOP Cognac

Yogurt Sauce*

Directions

Preheat oven to 400°F.

Mix thoroughly pork, lamb, bell pepper, onion, garlic, cilantro, cumin, cayenne pepper, cinnamon, cloves, cardamom, black pepper, and salt. Cover and refrigerate 2 hours.

Shape meat mixture into 12 meatballs. Place meatballs on parchment covered cookie sheet. Bake in oven for 15 to 20 minutes until lightly browned. Transfer meatballs to a heat-proof serving dish.

Tableside Service:

Place the serving dish with meatballs on a trivet. In a small saucepan or butter warmer on a rechaud on low heat, warm the VSOP Cognac.

Using a long match or wand lighter, ignite the alcohol in the saucepan or butter warmer. Start pouring a stream of flaming Cognac over the meatballs starting close to the meatballs and then rising for a dramatic effect of the flames.

Serve the meatballs with a yogurt sauce.

Scallops with Peach Chutney Bourbon Sauce

Serves 2

We are always looking for a new way to prepare and serve scallops. We took a bacon wrapped scallop recipe and did our spin. We live in California's central valley where fresh peaches are grown and are plentiful. We love to go to the u-pick orchard and gather peaches. We believe this is the perfect summertime recipe and will be a perfect addition to your repertoire when peaches come in season. Light with sweet tenderness of the peach paired with the bacon savory side makes a wonderful dish.

*See "Supporting Cast" for Peach Chutney recipe (page161).

Ingredients

4 slices thin cut bacon

4 large (size 6-8 per pound) sea scallops, cleaned, dried with paper towels

Kosher salt and freshly ground black pepper

2 tablespoons avocado oil

2 tablespoons butter, divided

1/2 cup Peach Chutney*

2 ounces Bourbon Whiskey

Directions

Preheat oven to 425°F.

Arrange bacon slices, leaving space around each, on an oven safe rack placed inside a baking sheet. Bake 5 to 10 minutes depending on thickness, until edges of bacon begin to brown. It should still be pliable when removed from oven. Cool.

Wrap a slice of bacon around the outside edge of each scallop, trimming bacon to fit the scallop. Secure the bacon around the scallop with a 6-inch bamboo skewer, fitting 2 scallops to each skewer. Season each bacon wrapped scallops with salt and pepper. Place on a platter.

Tableside Service:

Place 12-inch skillet on a rechaud over medium flame heat, add oil and 1 tablespoon butter to skillet and melt butter. Once the butter is melted and bubbling, place the scallops in the skillet and sear the scallops for 2 to 3 minutes on each side depending on scallop thickness. Transfer 2 scallops to each plate or scallop shell.

Add peach chutney to the skillet and heat; add remaining 1 tablespoon butter. Pull skillet back to heat front of skillet, pour Bourbon into front of skillet and heat Bourbon 1 to 2 seconds, using long match or wand lighter ignite Bourbon, stir into the peach chutney until flames go out.

Drape sauce around scallops and serve.

An Unforgettable Customer

I would like to share a story with you about being a Flambé Chef and some of the customers Darrell and I would meet while working in an upscale restaurant. Now, we were used to the doctor, lawyer, politician and the occasional celebrity, but one night when Darrell and I were working at the Rodeway Inn in Springfield, Oregon someone more interesting came in.

The Maitre d' came over to Darrell and I and said, "We are closing early tonight for a special guest. Finish what you are doing, but don't take any new orders." This was very mysterious and had never happened before!

So, when the dining room was cleared and the last guest had departed, we were all asked to gather around a very large table in the dining room. At that table was seated a rather distinguished middle-aged man in a suit and tie. Dying with curiosity about what was going on we and the wait staff fixated on this gentleman, the Maitre d' finally introduced us to our guest.

Darrell and I were about to meet our first Diamond Broker. As our Maitre d' introduced him, the man reached into his breast pocket and pulled a large velvet satchel out. He then proceeded to pour the contents out on the tablecloth. There in the middle of the table was a two-foot long and two-inch wide line of diamonds, emeralds, rubies, sapphires, and other precious stones.

Well, needless to say the staff were in awe! The man was in town to call on jewelry stores in the Eugene and Springfield area. He explained what he did for a living and if anyone was interested, he would sell the stones at a discount. This person definitely was one of the most interesting people we ever encountered in our careers.

Act II ~ Entrées

The entrées are more than just the second act, this is where the guest finds the stars of the show in all their glory. This act captivates your guest or guests with dazzling flames while exciting their senses with tantalizing flavors and ingredients.

Prawns Gargantua

Ragin' Cajun Prawns

Flaming Prawns in a Bourbon
Tomato Cream Sauce

Flaming Prawns Diablo

Scallops Flambé

Crab Legs Voltaire

Crab Legs Voltaire II

Lobster Thermidor

Stuffed Chicken Breasts with
Mango Chutney Sauce

Act II ~ Entrées

Brandied Chicken

Chicken Livers Supreme

Flamed Duck Breast à l'Orange

Flamed Duck Breast à l'Dark Sweet
Cherry Sauce

Steak Diane

Delmonico's Inspired Steak Diane

Tournedos of Beef

Châteaubriand Bouquètiere

Steak Au Poivre

Veal Scallops with Cognac Mushroom
Sauce

Act II ~ Entrées

Continued

Veal Chops with Cognac Cream Sauce

Pork Medallions with Cherry Infused
Sauce

Pork Medallions with Apples &
Calvados

Pork Chops with Flaming Apricot
Bourbon Sauce

Lamb Chops with Cognac & Cherry
Demi-Glace

Flamed Lamb Chops

Lollipop Lamb Chops with Cherry
Sauce

Entrées

Prawns Gargantua

Serves 2

This was one of the most popular dishes that I prepared at the Eugene Hotel. I think customers thought of it as being a healthy entrée as it was prawns but there is nothing low calorie about prawns in a spicy, butter sauce.

This is the first recipe I made for my future wife, Kathy, when we met and it has become one of her all-time favorites. She'll make a French baguette so we can dunk the warm bread into the glistening, spicy butter sauce that is to die for. This is a very easy and quick recipe to prepare with a delicious end result.

Ingredients

8 tablespoons butter

2 cloves garlic, minced

1 pound (size U/15 per pound) black tiger prawns, peeled and deveined

1 teaspoon paprika

1/2 teaspoon cayenne pepper

4 ounces Dry Sack Medium Sherry

Directions

Tableside Service:

Place a 12-inch skillet on a rechaud over medium flame heat, add butter to skillet and melt. Add garlic and sauté 1 minute. Add prawns in a single layer and sprinkle the paprika and cayenne over the prawns.

Cook, undisturbed, about 90 seconds, turn prawns and cook another 90 seconds until prawns are pink.

Pull prawns back towards the skillet handle, pull skillet back to heat front of the skillet, pour warmed sherry into the front of the skillet and heat 1 to 2 seconds, using a long match or wand lighter ignite the sherry and stir sherry into sauce until flames go out.

Serve the prawns and butter sherry sauce in bowls with a loaf of baguette to soak up the incredible butter sauce.

Ragin' Cajun Prawns

Serves 2

I have fond memories of growing up in the south and enjoying southern cookin'. This recipe is an homage to my Cajun roots as my father's family immigrated into the United States through the Port of New Orleans.

If you love spicy food, this recipe is for you! The cayenne pepper gives it a nice kick. If you want more heat, just increase the cayenne. Serve the prawns with a baguette, a big green salad and, a southern tradition, ice cold sweet tea.

Ingredients

1 teaspoon paprika

3/4 teaspoon freshly ground black pepper

1/4 teaspoon kosher salt

1/4 teaspoon dried oregano

1/4 teaspoon dried thyme

1/8 teaspoon cayenne pepper

1/4 teaspoon red pepper flakes

1 pound (size U/15 per pound) black tiger prawns, peeled and deveined

2 tablespoons avocado oil

4 tablespoons butter, cut into 2 tablespoon chunks

4 garlic cloves, finely minced

1 shallot, finely minced

3 tablespoons Worcestershire sauce

1 tablespoon freshly squeezed lemon juice

Zest of one-half lemon

2 ounces VSOP Cognac

Directions

In a small bowl, mix together the paprika, black pepper, salt, oregano, thyme, cayenne pepper, and red pepper flakes. Add the prawns to the seasoning and stir to coat.

Tableside Service:

Place a 12-inch skillet on a rechaud over medium flame heat; add and heat avocado oil and 2 tablespoons of butter until foaming. Stir in the garlic, shallot, Worcestershire sauce, lemon juice, and lemon zest. Sauté 1 to 2 minutes, until the garlic and shallot have softened. Add the prawns and sauté until they just turn pink, about 90 seconds per side.

Use a fork to pull the prawns back towards the skillet handle, pull skillet back to heat the front, pour Cognac into front of skillet and heat front 1 to 2 seconds, and use a long match or wand lighter to light the Cognac. Stir Cognac into the sauce until flames go out.

Turn off the burner flame and stir in the remaining 2 tablespoons butter until melted.

Serve in bowls or another option is to serve over sauteed okra, onion and tomatoes.

Flaming Prawns in a Bourbon Tomato Cream Sauce

Serves 2

The Roma tomatoes are a wonderful touch in this recipe. Their meatiness holds up to sautéing and the pecans add a pleasing crunch. The chives add a spot of onion taste without overwhelming the other flavors.

See "Supporting Cast" for the Sweet & Spicy Candied Pecans recipe (page 162).

Ingredients

1 tablespoon avocado oil

4 tablespoons butter

2 Roma tomatoes, diced

1/2 teaspoon kosher salt

1/4 teaspoon freshly ground black pepper

1/2 cup heavy whipping cream

1 pound (size U-15 per pound) black tiger prawns, peeled and deveined

2 ounces Bourbon Whiskey

1 tablespoon minced fresh chives

1/4 cup Sweet & Spicy Candied Pecans*

Directions

Tableside Service:

Place a 12-inch skillet on a rechaud over medium-high heat, melt together the avocado oil and butter. Add Roma tomatoes, sauté 2 to 3 minutes. Add salt, pepper, and cream and bring to a boil, reduce heat to a simmer.

Add prawns in a single layer and simmer 2 to 3 minutes, turn prawns over and simmer an additional 1 to 2 minutes until the prawns are pink.

Pull prawns back towards skillet handle, heat front of skillet, pour bourbon into front of skillet and heat 1 to 2 seconds, ignite Bourbon whiskey with a long match or wand lighter, and stir Bourbon whiskey into sauce until flames go out. Spoon sauce over prawns.

Serve prawns and sauce immediately over rice and garnish with chives and candied pecans.

Flaming Prawns Diablo

Serves 2

The South meets Mexico with this recipe. Sweet, spicy, smoky, salty, toasty, nutty, and creamy describes this recipe. The ingredients combine and you get this sweet smoky gentle heat, combined with the prawns that marries these flavors together and makes this recipe rock! Then you top the dish with pecans for a textural contrast and you have a winner.

Ingredients

2 tablespoons butter

2 tablespoons avocado oil

1 garlic clove, minced

1 pound (size U/15 per pound) black tiger prawns, peeled and deveined

2 ounces Bourbon Whiskey

1/2 cup heavy whipping cream

1 tablespoon chipotle adobo sauce

1 large chipotle pepper, minced

2 tablespoons honey

1/2 teaspoon kosher salt

1/4 cup chopped, toasted pecan halves

Directions

Tableside Service:

Place a 12-inch skillet on a rechaud over medium flame heat. Melt 1 tablespoon butter and the avocado oil together in the skillet; add garlic, lightly sauté 1 minute or less. Add prawns and sauté for 2 to 3 minutes then turn and sauté another 1 to 2 minutes until the prawns are firm and pink.

Use the fork to pull prawns back towards the skillet handle, pull skillet back to heat front, pour Bourbon whiskey into the front of the skillet and heat front for 1 to 2 seconds, light Bourbon whiskey with a long match or wand lighter. Stir Bourbon whiskey into sauce until flames go out.

Add heavy cream, chipotle adobo sauce, minced chipotle pepper, honey and salt; bring to a boil for 2 to 3 minutes and reduce to a sauce consistency coating the spoon. Turn off the rechaud and finish sauce by swirling in the remaining 1 tablespoon butter. Spoon sauce over the prawns.

Serve prawns and sauce over rice or in a bowl, top with chopped, toasted pecans.

Scallops Flambé

Serves 2

When scallops are prepared perfectly, the texture is buttery and the flavor mildly sweet. Some scallops may come with the side muscle still attached, just pull this off or use a paring knife to remove. Milk will help tenderize your scallops and remove their fishy taste, odor, and sand. Quickly rinse them with cold water, soak them for 30 minutes in milk, drain the scallops, and then blot them dry with paper towels. Dry scallops will sear to a golden brown.

Ingredients

10 large (size 6-8 per pound) sea scallops

2 tablespoons butter

3 tablespoons minced shallots

2 cloves garlic, minced

1/4 cup dry white wine

2 ounces VSOP Cognac

1/2 cup heavy whipping cream

1/4 cup freshly shredded Parmesan cheese

Kosher salt and freshly ground black pepper to taste

1 tablespoon chopped fresh Italian parsley

Directions

Pat scallops dry with a paper towel and place on decorative plate.

Tableside Service:

Place a 12-inch skillet on a rechaud over medium flame heat. Add butter to skillet and heat until bubbling; add the scallops and sauté 2 to 3 minutes per side. Remove scallops and reserve. Add the shallots and sauté until shallots are translucent. Add garlic and sauté 1 minute. Deglaze skillet with white wine.

Pull skillet back to heat front of skillet, pour Cognac into the front of the skillet and heat for 1 to 2 seconds, with long match or wand lighter ignite Cognac, stir until flames go out. Stir in heavy cream and Parmesan cheese, simmer until thickened. Season sauce with salt and pepper to taste. Return scallops to the skillet to reheat for about 1 minute, basting with the cream sauce.

Serve scallops over a bed of rice or orzo and garnish with chopped parsley

Crab Legs Voltaire

Serves 2

Early in 1904 at the St. Francis Hotel in San Francisco, Crab Legs Voltaire was invented or at least a version of it was introduced. When Victor Hirtzler, Executive Chef, opened the St. Francis dining room, he had on his menu Crayfish Voltaire; then, somewhere down the road crayfish went to Dungeness crab.

Though no one knows who exactly invented the recipe, the style is one that is reminiscent of Chef Escoffier and chefs of that era. This makes me hypothesize, with the help of the Westin St. Francis Hotel Historian, Howard Mutz, that the recipe was probably developed by Victor Hirtzler or, at least, he certainly influenced who created it. Remember, the fishing fleet would come into San Francisco and they would be loaded with fresh Dungeness crab. The St. Francis' proximity to the docks and having one of the most renowned Chefs in the world, it only makes sense that the Chef would come up with the recipe.

Chef Hirtzler's recipe from 1904 is, "Crab in chafing dish. Mince a shallot onion and brown slightly with two spoonful's of butter. Add a spoonful of flour, mixing well, then add a half pint of sweet milk, and stir to a smooth cream. Add the meat of a California crab (or six eastern crabs) and a tablespoonful of sherry. Place toast, cut in fancy shapes, on a deep platter, and cover with the crab. This is a favorite way of preparing crab."

I have included three recipes for you to try, Chef Hirtzler's recipe above, the one I prepared at the Eugene Hotel, and one Kathy created to be low in carbohydrates for a diabetic.

Ingredients

4 tablespoons butter

4 large white mushrooms, cleaned, trimmed, and sliced

1 1/2 ounces VSOP Cognac

2 tablespoons all-purpose flour

1 1/2 cups half and half

2 dashes Worcestershire sauce

2 dashes Tabasco sauce

1/4 teaspoon dry mustard

1/4 teaspoon kosher salt

1/4 teaspoon white pepper

1 ounce Dry Sack Medium Sherry

2 green onions, chopped

3/4 pound Dungeness crab legs and body meat or Alaska King crab leg meat cut into 2-inch pieces

Toast points, rice, or puff pastry

Directions

Tableside Service:

Place 12-inch skillet on a rechaud over medium flame heat; melt 2 tablespoons butter, add mushrooms and sauté about 3 minutes.

Using a fork, pull mushrooms back towards the handle, pull skillet back to heat front of skillet, pour Cognac into the front of the skillet and heat 1 to 2 seconds, with a long match or wand lighter ignite Cognac. Stir Cognac and mushrooms together until the flames go out.

Pull mushrooms back towards skillet handle, add remaining 2 tablespoons butter to the skillet, stir flour into butter to make a roux. Stir half and half into the roux; bring to a boil for 1 minute to thicken cream sauce. Reduce rechaud to low flame heat. Add Worcestershire sauce, Tabasco sauce, dry mustard, salt, pepper and sherry to the sauce. Gently fold in 3/4 of the green onions and crab legs, heat 2 to 3 minutes.

Serve over toast points, rice or puff pastry with a sprinkle of green onions on top.

Crab Legs Voltaire II

Serves 2

The West Coast is spoiled as we have the privilege to access one of the true delicacies of the world, Dungeness crab! This recipe is decadently rich combining the sweetness of the Dungeness crab, complimented by dry sherry in a rich, custard cream sauce.

This recipe is ideal for a diabetic or someone avoiding carbohydrates...unfortunately, though, this is not a low-fat recipe. Sometimes, you just have to indulge in a decadent meal.

No matter which Crab Legs Voltaire recipe you prepare, you will love it!

Ingredients

2 tablespoons butter

4 large white mushrooms, cleaned, trimmed, and sliced

1 1/2 ounces VSOP Cognac

4 egg yolks

1 1/2 cups heavy whipping cream

2 dashes Worcestershire sauce

2 dashes Tabasco sauce

1/4 teaspoon dry mustard

1/4 teaspoon kosher salt

1/4 teaspoon white pepper

1 ounce Dry Sack Medium Sherry

2 green onions, chopped

3/4 pound Dungeness crab legs and body meat or Alaska King crab leg meat cut into 2-inch pieces

Toast points, rice, or puff pastry

Directions

Tableside Service:

Place 12-inch skillet on a rechaud over medium flame heat; add and melt butter. Add mushrooms and sauté about 3 minutes.

Using a fork, pull mushrooms back towards the handle, pull skillet back to heat the front of skillet, pour Cognac into the front of the skillet and heat 1 to 2 seconds, with long match or wand lighter ignite Cognac, stir until the flame goes out.

Whisk egg yolks into cream and pour into the skillet. Simmer sauce, *do not boil*, for 3 to 4 minutes until sauce thickens and coats a spoon. Add Worcestershire sauce, Tabasco sauce, dry mustard, salt, pepper, and sherry to the sauce. Gently fold in 3/4 of the green onions and crab legs into the sauce, heat sauce 2 to 3 minutes.

Serve over toast points, rice, or puff pastry with a sprinkle of green onions.

Lobster Thermidor

Serves 2

Lobster Thermidor was possibly created and introduced on January 24th, 1891 at Chez Marie, a well-known Paris restaurant. On the evening of January 24, 1891, Victorien Sardou's play "Thermidor" had its first performance at the theatre called Comedie-Francais. Marie decided to launch his new dish by giving it the name of the play "Thermidor." That's the history, but it does not do this recipe justice!

Among lobster dishes, lobster thermidor stands out for its rich, savory, and indulgent flavor and is downright delicious. I hope you enjoy this dish as much as we do.

*See "Supporting Cast" section for Thermidor Lobster Stock (page 163), Thermidor Mushrooms (page 164), and Lobster Thermidor Sauce (page 165) recipes.

Ingredients

4 lobster tails, 6 ounces each

2 tablespoons butter

1 1/2 ounces VSOP Cognac

1 1/2 cups Lobster Thermidor Sauce*

8 ounces Thermidor Mushrooms*

Paprika

Directions

Shell lobster tails, reserve shells for Lobster Stock*, and cut meat into bite-sized pieces.

Prepare the Thermidor Lobster Stock and Thermidor Mushrooms for the Thermidor Sauce, then prepare Thermidor Sauce. Place mushrooms in a decorative bowl and pour sauce into a decorative pitcher.

Tableside Service:

Place a 12-inch skillet on a rechaud over medium flame heat. Melt butter in skillet; add lobster pieces and sauté 2 to 3 minutes until the lobster turns pink.

Using a fork, pull lobster meat back towards skillet handle, pull skillet back to heat front of skillet, pour Cognac into front of skillet and heat Cognac 1 to 2 seconds, using long match or wand lighter ignite Cognac. Stir sauce and Cognac together until flames are out.

Add thermidor sauce and thermidor mushrooms and gently fold lobster into the sauce. Allow to simmer 2 to 3 minutes.

Stuffed Chicken Breasts with Mango Chutney Sauce

Serves 2

One night my wife and I were playing around in the kitchen and came up with this recipe. I love the touch in the recipe where we roll up the stuffed chicken breasts in film wrap to tightly seal in the goat cheese. When we cooked the chicken breast rolls, the goat cheese stayed where it was supposed to be inside the breast and not oozing all over the skillet.

*See "Supporting Cast" for the Mango Chutney recipe (page 166).

Ingredients

2 6-ounce boneless, skinless chicken breasts

Kosher salt and freshly ground black pepper

4 ounces goat cheese, formed into 2 2-inch-long logs

2 tablespoons avocado oil

4 tablespoons butter

1/2 cup Mango Chutney*

2 ounces VSOP Cognac

Directions

Place a chicken breast between two layers of plastic wrap or wax paper. Using a meat mallet's flat side, pound evenly until the breast is a scant 1/4 inch thick. Repeat with the remaining breast. Season the inside of the breasts with salt and pepper. Place a goat cheese log in the middle of each breast, fold sides of chicken over goat cheese, then form chicken breast into a large roll.

Roll out a long sheet of plastic wrap at least twice as long as the chicken breast roll. Place chicken roll on the middle edge of sheet of plastic wrap and roll up chicken in the wrap. Take ends of wrap and twist to tightly seal chicken breast; chill chicken breasts. Prior to tableside service, unwrap the chicken logs and place on a decorative plate.

Tableside Service:

Place a 12-inch skillet on a rechaud over medium heat, add oil and heat to shimmering. Place chicken breasts seam side down in skillet to seal in the filling. Sauté chicken, browning the sides of the chicken, for about 10 minutes. Add Mango Chutney and the butter, scraping up chicken bits.

Pull chicken rolls back towards skillet handle, pull skillet back to heat front of skillet, pour Cognac into front of skillet and heat 1 to 2 seconds, ignite Cognac using long match or wand lighter and stir Cognac into the chutney sauce until flames are gone.

Place chicken rolls on a plate and spoon the sauce over the rolls.

Brandied Chicken

Serves 2

My wife and I make this recipe with Chanterelles, a golden, rich, meaty mushroom that grows in the Pacific Northwest Sitka spruce forests. If using chanterelles, clean carefully as the spruce needles manage to end up inside the mushrooms. As fresh Chanterelles are only available for a short period in the fall every year, we have also used brown cremini mushrooms, that way I can make Brandied Chicken more often. Trust me, you are going to love this recipe!

Ingredients

2 6-ounce boneless, skinless chicken breasts or thighs

2 tablespoons avocado oil

2 tablespoons butter

8 ounces chanterelle or cremini mushrooms, cleaned, trimmed, and sliced

2 cloves garlic, minced

2 ounces VSOP Cognac

1/2 cup heavy whipping cream

1/4 teaspoon kosher salt

1/8 teaspoon freshly ground black pepper

Directions

Place the chicken breasts between 2 sheets of wax paper and gently pound them to a uniform thickness of 1/4-inch. Season chicken breasts with salt and pepper on both sides, place on plate.

Tableside Service:

Place a 12-inch skillet on a rechaud over medium flame heat, add and heat avocado oil until shimmering. Add chicken to the skillet and cook 2 to 3 minutes per side, or until juices run clear, turning a golden brown. Remove to a platter.

Add the 2 tablespoons of butter and mushrooms to the skillet, sauté 2 to 3 minutes until mushrooms are tender. Add garlic and sauté 1 minute.

Using the fork, pull mushrooms and garlic back towards the skillet handle, pull skillet back to heat front of skillet, pour Cognac into front of skillet and heat 1 to 2 seconds, and using long match or wand lighter ignite Cognac. As the flames go out, add cream, salt and pepper and simmer 3 to 4 minutes to reduce to a sauce consistency.

Serve mushroom sauce over chicken with potatoes, pasta, rice or polenta.

Chicken Livers Supreme

Serves 2

I hate liver, but I love chicken liver pâté! The flavor of Chicken Livers Supreme is very similar to my wife's chicken liver pâté. This recipe might be old school recipe from the 1960's but it is definitely fine dining on a budget!

Serving the chicken livers and sherry sauce over rice with a glass of dry sherry really completes the meal.

Ingredients

1 cup milk

1/2 pound chicken livers

4 tablespoons butter

1 tablespoon all-purpose flour

1 clove garlic, minced

1/2 teaspoon white pepper

1/2 teaspoon kosher salt

1/4 teaspoon freshly ground nutmeg

1 teaspoon minced fresh thyme

1 cup half & half

2 ounces Dry Sack Medium Sherry

2 green onions chopped

Directions

Rinse chicken livers with water and trim livers of fat and connective tissue. Place the livers in a bowl and cover with milk and refrigerate for 2 to 3 hours to tenderize the livers and mellow any strong, bitter flavors. Remove livers from refrigerator, drain milk, rinse with cold water, and pat dry. Place in a decorative bowl.

Tableside Service:

Place a 12-inch skillet on a rechaud over medium flame heat; melt butter in skillet. To make a roux, reduce heat to low, stir flour into butter and add garlic, pepper, salt, nutmeg, and thyme. Stir in half & half, increase heat to medium-high to thicken sauce, about 3 to 4 minutes.

Once sauce is thickened, add chicken livers. Using a spoon, gently turn the chicken livers in the sauce, cooking about 5 minutes or until the blood rises from the livers. Gently fold in the sherry and half of the green onions.

Serve over steamed rice or toast points and garnish with remaining green onions.

Flamed Duck Breasts à l'Orange or à l'Dark Sweet Cherry Sauce

Serves 2

Pan seared duck breast meat is the most tender and succulent piece of duck and is an exquisite delicacy.

Starting the duck breasts in a cold skillet gives time for the fat to render and the skin to become a crispy culinary delight. The duck breasts are best served medium-rare to retain its flavor and texture. Finishing the duck breasts with the flavorful, savory cherry sauce or the classic citrusy orange sauce enhances the duck and is sure to impress your guest.

See "Supporting Cast" for the Orange Sauce (page 167) or Dark Sweet Cherry Sauce (168) recipes.

Ingredients

1 pound double lobe duck breast, separated into 2 lobes, each about 8 ounces

Kosher salt to taste

1 1/2 ounces VSOP Cognac

Orange or Dark Sweet Cherry Sauce*

1 tablespoon butter

Directions

Pat duck breasts dry. With a sharp knife, gently score duck breast skin in a tight crosshatch pattern, keeping the scores 1/2 inch apart, taking care not to expose the flesh.

Generously season with salt and rub into each breast. Let rest, skin-side up, at room temperature, for 15 minutes.

Prepare orange or dark sweet cherry sauce, place in a decorative pitcher.

Tableside Service:

Place a 12-inch skillet on a rechaud; place duck breast lobes skin side down into the cold skillet. Turn rechaud on to a medium flame heat and cook duck breasts 4 to 6 minutes until skin has turned a dark, golden brown and is crispy.

As the duck cooks, spoon fat into another dish, save fat for future use. Flip duck breasts and cook until they start to firm and are reddish-pink and juicy in the center, about 4 minutes more. An instant-read thermometer inserted into the center should read 125° F. Transfer breasts to a carving board to rest.

Pull skillet back to heat the front, pour Cognac into front of the skillet and heat 1 to 2 seconds, using a long match or wand ignitor ignite Cognac. Stir Cognac to bring up bits of browned duck.

À l'Orange Service: Pour orange sauce into skillet, gently heat 2 to 3 minutes. Turn off heat, stir butter into the sauce.

À l'Dark Sweet Cherry Service: Pour cherry sauce into the skillet, gently heat 2 to 3 minutes. Turn off heat, stir butter into the sauce.

Presentation: Slice duck breasts across the grain, arrange on a plate, and spoon orange or cherry sauce over the top.

Steak Diane

Serves 2

There are a number of speculations as to the exact origin of Steak Diane. Some say that it was named after the Roman Goddess of the hunt "Diana" and was invented by Chef Auguste Escoffier in 1909. However, that recipe looks nothing like the recipe I make! Another version is Tony Clerici's.

In 1938 Clerici invented the recipe when he worked at the Mayfair Hotel in London at a restaurant named Tony's Grill and then named it after a prominent British Socialite named Lady Diana Cooper. Now, that version looks a lot like the version I make. No matter who developed this recipe or when, Steak Diane is an elegant entrée made delicious by the caramelization process of the flambé.

Ingredients

4 tablespoons butter

1/2 pound mushrooms, cleaned, trimmed, and sliced 1/4-inch thick

1 tablespoon avocado oil

4 3-ounce tenderloin steak medallions, 1-inch thick

2 ounces VSOP Cognac

1/4 cup prepared Minor's Au Jus Prep Beef

1/4 cup A.1. Steak Sauce

3 green onions, chopped

Directions

Tableside Service:

Place a 12-inch skillet on a rechaud over medium flame heat, add butter to skillet and melt butter. Add mushrooms, cook until softened, about 3 minutes.

Using a fork, pull mushrooms to the back of the skillet to allow space for the steaks. Pour oil into the front of the skillet and add the steaks, sauté steaks to desired doneness:

• *Rare* - cook 3 minutes, turn; cook 1 more minute.
• *Medium-rare* - cook until blood rises to the top of steak, turn and cook 1 more minute for medium well.
• *Well-done* - first in skillet, cook until blood rises to top of the steaks, turn and cook 2 more minutes.

As the steaks finish cooking move steak medallions to rest on top of the mushrooms.

Pull skillet back to heat front, pour Cognac into the front of skillet and heat 1 to 2 seconds, using a long match or wand lighter ignite Cognac, and stir Cognac into the sauce until flames are gone.

Add beef au jus, A.1. sauce, and green onions to the front of the skillet and reduce sauce 2 to 3 minutes. Stir sauce and mushrooms together while spooning over the steaks.

Serve 2 medallions on each plate with mushroom sauce and a light garnish of chopped green onions.

Delmonico's Inspired Steak Diane

Serves 2

This is a version of the Emeril Lagasse recipe for Delmonico's in New Orleans. Kathy and I did make some minor changes to his recipe. So, this is our version of the classic recipe.

Ingredients

1/2 cup water

2 tablespoons Minor's Demi Glace Concentrate

4 (3-ounce) tenderloin steak, medallions, 1-inch thick

Kosher salt and freshly ground black pepper

2 tablespoons avocado oil

1 tablespoon butter

8 ounces mushrooms, cleaned, trimmed, and sliced 1/4-thick

1 shallot, minced

1 garlic clove, minced

2 ounces VSOP Cognac

1/2 cup heavy whipping cream

2 teaspoons Dijon mustard

2 teaspoons Worcestershire sauce

3 green onions, chopped

1 teaspoon minced chervil, French parsley, or Italian parsley

Directions

Place water in a microwaveable container and heat 1 minute in microwave. Stir in the demi-glace concentrate.

Generously season the steak medallions with salt and pepper, place on a decorative plate.

Tableside Service:

Place a 12- inch skillet on a rechaud over medium flame heat, add avocado oil and 1 tablespoon butter; melt butter. Add mushrooms, cook until softened, about 2 to 3 minutes. Add shallots and garlic to skillet and sauté 1 minute.

Using a fork, pull mushrooms, shallots, and garlic to the back of the skillet, pull skillet back to heat front of skillet, pour Cognac into front of skillet and heat 1 to 2 seconds, using a long match or wand lighter ignite Cognac, and stir Cognac until flames are gone.

Add steaks to the front of the skillet, sauté steaks until desired doneness:

• *Rare*, cook 3 minutes, turn; cook 1 more minute.
• *Medium-rare*, cook until blood rises to the top of steak, turn and cook 1 more minute for medium well.
• *Well-done*, first in skillet, cook until blood rises to top of the steaks, turn and cook 2 more minutes.

When steaks are done cooking, pull steaks from front of skillet and place on the mushrooms to rest.

Add to skillet the heavy cream, prepared demi-glace, Worcestershire sauce, Dijon mustard, 3/4 of the green onions and parsley. Stir sauce and mushrooms together and spoon mushroom sauce over the steaks.

Serve 2 medallions on each plate with mushroom sauce draped over the top and sprinkle on the remaining green onions.

Tournedos of Beef

Serves 2

It's French, decadent and I love the different sauce choices! This is French cooking at its best. Tournedos of Beef are served with the classic French sauce(s) Bordelaise, Champignon or Chasseur, also known as a Hunter Sauce. The Bordelaise is a smooth red wine sauce, the Champignon is a beefy mushroom sauce, and the Chasseur is a rich tomato flavored sauce. No matter which sauce you choose, it will be a wonderful accompaniment for your tenderloin steak.

*See "Supporting Cast" for the Champignon (page 170), Chasseur (page 171), or Bordelaise Sauce (page 169) recipes.

Ingredients

2 beef tenderloin steaks,
6 ounces each

Kosher salt and freshly ground
black pepper

2 tablespoons avocado oil

2 ounces VSOP Cognac

2 tablespoons butter

Champignon, Chasseur, or
Bordelaise Sauce*

Directions

Prepare your choice of sauce and place in a pitcher.

Tableside Service:

Season the tenderloins with salt and pepper.

Place a 12-inch skillet on a rechaud over medium flame heat; add oil and heat until shimmering. Add tenderloins to the skillet; sear the tenderloins until desired doneness:

• *Rare*, cook 3 minutes, turn; cook 1 more minute.
• *Medium-rare*, cook until blood rises to the top of steak, turn and cook 1 more minute for medium well.
• *Well-done*, first in skillet, cook until blood rises to top of the steaks, turn and cook 2 more minutes.

Using a fork, pull tenderloins back towards skillet handle. Pull skillet back to heat front of skillet, pour Cognac into front of skillet and heat 1 to 2 seconds, using a long match or wand lighter ignite Cognac, and stir Cognac into the sauce until flames are gone. Swirl in the butter and baste the steaks with the Cognac butter sauce.

Remove the tenderloins from the skillet, to two warm plates. Serve with a Champignon, Chasseur, or Bordelaise Sauce.

Châteaubriand Bouquètiere

Serves 2

It is speculated that the dish Chateaubriand was created and named for the French writer and politician François-René de Chateaubriand in the early 1820's by the namesake's personal chef, Montmireil.

Chateaubriand started out as an entrée, then a restaurant menu item that became a specific cut of meat.

Chateaubriand is a large, tender cut of beef from the thickest section of the tenderloin. If two people want a presentation of a complete meal this is the way to go! This is a tableside presentation of a roasted beef tenderloin garnished with a colorful bouquet of vegetables and potatoes, and served with a Béarnaise sauce creating the perfect meal for a special occasion or holiday celebration.

A flambé presentation is to heat Cognac in a small saucepan or butter warmer, ignite the Cognac and then drizzle over the roasted beef tenderloin prior to carving.

*See "Supporting Cast" for Roasted Beef Tenderloin (page 172), Roasted Tomato Half Crowns (page 173), Duchess Potatoes (page 174), Béarnaise Sauce (page 175) and Bordelaise Sauce (page 169) recipes.

Ingredients

1 center cut, 2 to 3 pound, Roasted Beef Tenderloin*

2 Roasted Tomato Half Crowns*

10 steamed asparagus spears, buttered

2 mounds Duchess Potatoes*

1 1/2 ounces VSOP Cognac, *optional*

1 cup Béarnaise or Bordelaise Sauce*

Directions

On a large, warmed presentation platter, place the tenderloin in the middle of the platter.

On opposite corners of the platter, place a roasted tomato half. On the other opposite corners of the platter, place a duchess potato mound. To each side of the tenderloin place the asparagus spears.

Tableside Service:

If presenting a flaming tenderloin, light the Cognac and begin drizzling the flaming Cognac over the top of the beef then, with flair, raise up the butter warmer about 12-inches above the roast for a fountain of flame.

Carve the tenderloin into slices. Place on each dinner plates 3 slices of tenderloin, a tomato, the asparagus, and the duchess potatoes.

Serve with béarnaise or bordelaise sauce.

Steak Au Poivre

Serves 2

According to French steak specialist Francis Marie, Steak Au Poivre originated in the 19th century in the bistros of Normandy, where noted figures took their female companions for late suppers, and where pepper's purported aphrodisiac properties may have proved most useful. This may or may not be historically accurate unless you believe that it was probably invented by Auguste Escoffier and the sauce was originally intended to be used with venison. Chef Escoffier published the recipe in 1903 in "Le Guide Culinaire" and this is the version I would believe!

For the peppercorn coating, put the peppercorns into a zip lock bag and use a mallet to pound the peppercorns into a coarse, crunchy pepper coating. Using finely ground pepper will burn by the time the steak is done. I also coat only one side of steak with pepper so I can get a hard sear on the non-peppered side. I prefer to taste the tenderloin versus having a mouth full of burnt pepper.

Ingredients

4 tenderloin steaks, 4 ounces each, 1-inch thick

1 teaspoon kosher salt

1 tablespoon coarsely crushed black peppercorns

2 tablespoons avocado oil

2 tablespoons butter

1 shallot, minced

2 ounces VSOP Cognac

1 cup heavy whipping cream

1 teaspoon Dijon mustard

Directions

Pat tenderloin steaks dry with paper towels. Sprinkle steaks with salt. Put crushed pepper on a plate, press only one side of the steaks into the pepper to evenly coat. Allow steaks to rest for 15 minutes.

Tableside Service:

Place a 12-inch skillet on a rechaud over medium flame heat, add avocado oil and heat until shimmering. Add steaks, pepper side up; sear until desired doneness:

• *Rare,* hard sear 3 minutes, turn; cook 1 more minute.

• *Medium-rare,* sear until blood rises to the top of steak, turn and cook 1 more minute for medium well.

• *Well-done,* first in skillet, sear until blood rises to top of the steaks, turn and cook 2 more minutes.

Pull steaks from skillet and place on platter to rest. Lower the heat to low and add butter and shallot. Cook, stirring constantly, scraping up the brown bits, until the shallots are golden brown and softened, 2 to 3 minutes.

Pull skillet back to heat front, pour Cognac into front of skillet and heat 1 to 2 seconds, ignite with a long match or wand lighter, and stir until flames go out. Add cream and Dijon mustard and gently boil sauce until thickened and coats a spoon, about 3 minutes.

Transfer the steaks to plates and spoon sauce over the tops.

Veal Scallops with Cognac Mushroom Sauce

Serves 2

The French love their cream sauces and this recipe does not disappoint. When I think of French cooking I think of this recipe as it has veal, mushrooms, Cognac, butter, and cream. This entrée is designed for an elegant, formal dinner party!

Ingredients

4 veal scallops, about 4 ounces each

Kosher salt and freshly ground black pepper

2 tablespoons avocado oil

4 tablespoons butter

8 ounces brown cremini mushrooms, cleaned, trimmed, and sliced

2 cloves garlic, minced

2 ounces VSOP Cognac

3/4 cup heavy whipping cream

3 green onions, sliced

Directions

Place veal scallops on a decorative platter and season with salt and pepper.

Tableside Service:

Place a 12-inch skillet on a rechaud over medium-high flame heat; add oil and heat until shimmering. Add the veal scallops to the skillet and sear the veal, in batches if necessary, about 1 1/2 minutes each side. Transfer the veal to a platter.

Add the butter to the skillet; add and sauté mushrooms until softened. Add garlic and sauté 1 minute.

Using a fork, pull mushrooms back towards skillet handle, pull skillet back to heat front of skillet, pour Cognac into front of skillet and heat 1 to 2 seconds, using a long match or wand lighter ignite Cognac, stir into mushrooms until flames go out. Add cream and simmer for 5 minutes. Add veal scallops back into skillet and fold in 3/4 of the green onions.

Serve 2 veal scallops on a dinner plate, coat with mushroom cream sauce and a sprinkle of the remaining green onions.

Veal Chops with Cognac Cream Sauce

Serves 2

Veal chops are rated as one of my top meals. There are two different veal chops that may be used in this recipe. Veal rib chops are similar to a rib eye steak and veal porterhouse chops are similar to a t-bone steak, with the tenderloin on one side and strip loin on the other. Both chops are an excellent choice as they are both tender and succulent. Veal has a delicate flavor and this recipe's ingredients combine with the veal to make a rich cream sauce with the savory mushrooms, a hint of thyme, the sweet pungent flavor of the shallots, and Cognac character.

Ingredients

1/4 cup boiling water

2 teaspoons Minor's Demi Glace Sauce Concentrate

2 16-ounce veal chops, rib or porterhouse

Kosher salt and freshly ground black pepper

2 tablespoons avocado oil

8 ounces mushrooms, cleaned, trimmed, and sliced

2 large shallots, minced

2 tablespoons butter

2 ounces VSOP Cognac

1/4 cup chicken stock

1/2 cup heavy whipping cream

2 teaspoons minced thyme

Directions

Stir demi-glace concentrate into the boiling water and pour into a decorative pitcher or bowl.

Generously season veal chops with salt and pepper.

Tableside Service:

Place a 12-inch skillet on a rechaud over medium flame heat, add avocado oil to skillet and heat until shimmering. Add veal chops to skillet and sear 4 to 5 minutes on each side or until golden brown. To check for doneness, press the veal with the back of the fork – if the meat feels spongy under pressure, it needs further cooking. When the veal loses that resilience and is firm to touch, it is done, remove chops to plates and set aside to rest.

Add mushrooms, shallots and butter to skillet and sauté until mushrooms are softened.

Pull mushrooms back towards skillet handle, pull skillet back to heat front of skillet, pour Cognac into front of skillet and heat 1 to 2 seconds, ignite with a long match or wand lighter, as flames go out stir Cognac into the sauce.

Stir chicken stock, cream, demi-glace sauce and thyme into the mushroom sauce. Bring sauce to a boil and reduce sauce until it coats a spoon, about 3 to 5 minutes.

Ladle sauce onto a plate or platter, place chop on top of sauce, and drizzle more sauce over the top. Serve chops and sauce with mashed potatoes.

Pork Medallions with Cherry Infused Sauce

Serves 2

This is the recipe for someone who is on a budget and wants to entertain and serve an elegant meal! Easy to make with a great blend of flavors with nothing being dominate. The spices being rolled around the pork tenderloin, the pork seared to a golden brown and topped with a cherry sauce makes for a beautiful presentation.

Ingredients

1 whole pork tenderloin

1 teaspoon Herbes de Provence

1 teaspoon minced thyme leaves

1/4 teaspoon kosher salt

1/4 teaspoon freshly ground black pepper

1/4 cup dried cherries

2 ounces Sandeman Founder's Reserve Ruby Porto port wine

1/2 cup chicken stock

2 teaspoons Minor's Demi Glace Sauce Concentrate

1 1/2 tablespoons avocado oil

3 tablespoons butter, divided into 1 tablespoon and 2 tablespoons

2 medium shallots, finely chopped

2 medium cloves garlic, minced

2 ounces Schladerer Cherry Kirschwasser

Thyme sprigs

Directions

Trim the pork tenderloin to 6-inch length by removing the ends of the tenderloin, reserve ends for another dish. Place a sheet of plastic wrap on the counter, 3 inches longer at each end than the pork tenderloin, then place the pork in the center along the edge of the wrap. Mix together the Herbes de Provence, thyme, salt, and pepper and sprinkle half the mixture over the pork and roll over the pork and sprinkle on remaining seasonings. Roll up pork inside the plastic wrap and tightly twist ends of the wrap. Refrigerate pork overnight.

Place cherries in a decorative bowl and cover with the ruby port, set aside to macerate 3 to 4 hours.

Bring pork loin out to room temperature for 30 minutes. Unwrap and cut the tenderloin crosswise into 1-inch thick slices, about 6 medallions and place on a decorative plate.

Place chicken stock into a microwaveable container, heat 2 minutes. Stir in demi-glace concentrate and transfer to a decorative pitcher.

Tableside Service:

Place a 12-inch skillet on a rechaud over medium-high flame heat. Add avocado oil and 1 tablespoon butter, heat until butter melts.

Add the pork medallions and sear on each side, about 2 minutes per side. Remove to 2 serving plates, let medallions rest.

Reduce rechaud heat to medium; add shallots and garlic and sauté until softened, about 1 to 2 minutes. Deglaze skilled with the cherries and port wine; add chicken stock and demi-glace concentrate and stir until slightly thickened.

Pull cherries back towards skillet handle, pull skillet back to heat front of skillet, pour Kirschwasser into the front of the skillet and heat 1 to 2 seconds, using a long match or wand lighter ignite the Kirschwasser, as flames go out stir Kirschwasser into the cherry sauce.

Add the remaining 2 tablespoons butter to the sauce and swirl in. Serve sauce over the medallions. Garnish with fresh thyme sprigs.

Pork Medallions with Apples & Calvados

Serves 2

This easy pork recipe showcases the flavors of Normandy, France - Calvados, apples, and cream. If French cooking is about the sauce and you want an entrée with apples and cream, you are going to love this recipe. The apples engage with the onions, Calvados, and cream to make a very light entrée with hints of sage, rosemary and thyme. You may substitute apple brandy but will lose the nuance of the Calvados with its apple and pear flavor. I prefer to use Granny Smith apples as they remain firm when cooked and their slightly tart flavor adds depth to the sauce.

If you don't include pork in your meals, veal scallops or chicken breasts are a great substitute for pork in this recipe.

Ingredients

3/4 pound boneless pork loin medallions, 3/4-inch thick, patted dry

Kosher salt and freshly ground black pepper

2 tablespoons avocado oil

2 tablespoons butter

2 shallots, finely chopped

1 Granny Smith Apple, peeled, cored thinly sliced

2 ounces Calvados Apple Brandy

1/4 cup chicken stock

1/4 cup apple juice

1/2 cup heavy whipping cream

1 teaspoon minced fresh sage

1 teaspoon minced fresh rosemary

1 teaspoon minced fresh thyme

4 whole sage leaves

Directions

Tableside Service:

Season pork medallions generously with salt and pepper.

Place a 12-inch skillet on a rechaud over medium flame heat, add avocado oil and heat until shimmering. Add pork and sear on each side until browned, about four minutes per side. Remove pork to a plate.

Add butter, shallots and apples to skillet, sauté until softened. Using a fork, pull shallots and apples back towards skillet handle, pull skillet back to heat front, pour Calvados into front of skillet and heat 1 to 2 seconds, using a long match or wand lighter ignite Calvados, when flames go out stir Calvados into the sauce.

Pour in chicken stock and apple juice, scraping up browned bits, and reduce liquid by half. Add cream, sage, rosemary and thyme, reduce to desired sauce consistency. Return pork loin medallions to skillet and spoon apples and sauce over the medallions. Divide pork between plates and spoon sauce over the top.

Garnish with sage leaves.

Pork Chops with Flaming Apricot Bourbon Sauce

Serves 2

This is another fast and easy recipe for you to prepare, while at the same time being elegant and wonderful tasting. Plus, pork loin is very cost effective item when looking at an entrée to serve if you need to watch those dollars!

Ingredients

2 boneless pork loin chops, 3/4-inch thick

1/2 teaspoon kosher salt

1/2 teaspoon freshly ground black pepper

1/2 teaspoon ground fennel seed

2 tablespoons avocado oil

2 tablespoons minced shallots

1 teaspoon minced garlic

1 tablespoon fresh lemon juice

1 tablespoon apple cider vinegar

1 tablespoon Dijon mustard

1/4 cup apricot preserves

2 tablespoons butter

1/4 cup chopped dried apricots

2 teaspoons fresh thyme leaves

2 ounces Bourbon Whiskey

Directions

Using a paper towel, blot chops dry. Mix together the kosher salt, freshly ground black pepper, and ground fennel and season both sides of each chop with the seasoning mixture; place chops on decorative plate.

Tableside Service:

Place a 12-inch skillet on a rechaud over medium flame heat, add avocado oil. When oil is shimmering, place the chops in the skillet. Sear chops on each side about 4 minutes per side. Transfer chops to a plate.

Reduce rechaud to low heat; add shallots and garlic and sauté until softened, about 1 to 2 minutes. Stir in lemon juice, apple cider vinegar, Dijon mustard, apricot preserves and 1 tablespoon butter to make a sauce. Stir in dried apricots and minced thyme.

Pull apricot sauce back towards skillet handle, pull skillet back to heat front of skillet, pour Bourbon whiskey into skillet and heat 1 to 2 seconds, using a long match or wand lighter ignite the Bourbon whiskey, as flames go out stir Bourbon whiskey into the sauce. Swirl in remaining 1 tablespoon butter. Return the chops back into the skillet and baste with sauce.

Serve chops with sauce and a sprinkle of thyme leaves.

Lamb Chops with Cognac & Cherry Demi-Glace

Serves 2

Use cherry preserves rather than jam for the sauce, as the preserves have large chunks of fruit. I prefer the Bonne Maman preserves brand as it adds an intense fruit flavor for my sauces! We think this recipe hits the right balance between sweet and savory and is a world class recipe.

Ingredients

1/4 cup water

2 teaspoons Minor's Demi Glace Sauce Concentrate

2 5-ounce bone-in loin lamb chops

Kosher salt and freshly ground black pepper

2 tablespoons avocado oil

1/4 cup cherry preserves

1/2 teaspoon minced rosemary

2 ounces VSOP Cognac

2 tablespoons butter

Directions

Add water to a microwaveable container and heat water in microwave for 30 seconds; stir in demi-glace concentrate, pour into a decorative pitcher.

Season lamb chops with kosher salt and black pepper.

Tableside Service:

Place a 12-inch skillet on a rechaud over medium flame heat; add avocado oil and heat until shimmering. Add lamb chops to skillet and sear until golden brown on each side, 3 to 4 minutes on both sides for rare, 120°F. Sauté longer for doneness as follows:

Medium-Rare - 125°F	Medium - 130°F
Medium-Well - 145°F	Well-Done - 150°F

Pull lamb chops from the skillet to a platter.

Add the demi-glace, cherry preserves and rosemary to skillet and stir together. Using a spoon pull sauce back towards skillet handle, pull skillet back to heat front of the skillet, pour Cognac into the front of the skillet and heat 1 to 2 seconds, using a long match or wand lighter ignite Cognac, and as flames go out stir Cognac into the cherry sauce. Swirl butter into sauce. Add lamb chops back into sauce and spoon sauce over the lamb,

Plate up lamb chops and pour cherry sauce over each serving.

Flamed Lamb Chops

Serves 2

The marinade helps this recipe in every way. First, the marinade is absorbed into the meat to impart its wonderful flavors. Then the marinade is added into the sauce to combine with the demi-glace, which adds richness to the sauce. Finally, the sauce is punctuated with the butter to give it a smoothness.

Ingredients

4 6-ounce bone-in loin lamb chops

2 tablespoons extra-virgin olive oil

2 tablespoons lemon juice

1/2 teaspoon Dijon mustard

2 to 3 dashes Worcestershire sauce

1/2 teaspoon kosher salt

1/2 teaspoon freshly ground black pepper

2 cloves garlic, finely minced

Dash of cayenne pepper

3/4 cup red wine

1/2 cup water

2 tablespoons Minor's Demi Glace Sauce Concentrate

2 tablespoons avocado oil

1 1/2 ounces VSOP Cognac

1 tablespoon butter

Directions

Place lamb chops in a large bowl. In a small bowl, mix together olive oil, lemon juice, Dijon mustard, Worcestershire sauce, salt, pepper, garlic, cayenne pepper, and red wine. Pour marinade over lamb chops; marinate at least 1 hour. Drain lamb chops, reserving 1/2 cup marinade for the final sauce, pat dry and place on decorative platter.

Heat water to boiling in microwave oven, about 1 minute; stir in demi-glace sauce concentrate, set aside in a decorative pitcher.

Tableside Service:

Place a 12-inch skillet on a rechaud over medium flame heat, add avocado oil and 1 tablespoon butter; melt butter. Add lamb chops and sear 3 to 4 minutes on both sides for rare, 120°F. Sauté longer for doneness as follows:

Medium-Rare - 125°F	Medium - 130°F
Medium-Well - 145°F	Well-Done - 150°F

Pull lamb chops from the skillet to a platter.

Pull skillet back to heat the front, pour Cognac into front of the skillet and heat 1 to 2 seconds, ignite Cognac with a long match or wand lighter, and as flames go out scrape up the fond or bits of caramelized meat. Stir in the demi-glace, the 1/2 cup reserved marinade, and 1 tablespoon butter into the sauce.

Serve lamb chops draped in sauce or with a bowl of sauce.

Lollipop Lamb Chops with Cherry Sauce

Serves 2

I have listed this recipe in two areas in this cookbook because people forget where they saw it! This recipe can be an excellent starter or center of the plate super star, it is up to you.

Ingredients

1/4 cup dried cherries

1 ounce Schladerer Cherry Kirshwasser

3/4 cup water

2 tablespoons Minor's Demi Glace Sauce Concentrate

4 lollipop lamb chops from Frenched rack of lamb

Kosher salt and freshly ground black pepper

2 tablespoons avocado oil

1 large shallot, finely chopped

2 ounces Schladerer Cherry Kirshwasser

1 teaspoon Worcestershire sauce

1 teaspoon Dijon mustard

1/2 cup cherry preserves

1 tablespoon butter

Directions

Place cherries in a small microwaveable dish; pour 2 tablespoons Cherry Kirschwasser over the cherries. Microwave 30 seconds, set aside.

Place the 3/4 cup water in a microwaveable container and heat 1 minute in microwave; stir in the demi-glace concentrate. Pour demi-glace sauce into a pitcher.

To French a rack of lamb; first, place a knife blade about a quarter of an inch above the eye of the lamb chop and cut a line from the first rib to the other end of the rack. Now, run the knife blade between the ribs and cut down to the first cut line and then across to the next rib and up the rib forming a U pattern, now clean the rib of fat. Take knife and cut the rib to make the chop.

Season lamb chops with salt and pepper.

Tableside Service:

Place a 12-inch skillet on a rechaud over medium flame heat; add avocado oil to skillet and heat until shimmering. Place lollipop lamb chops into the skillet and sear 3 to 4 minutes on both sides for rare, 120°F. Sauté longer for doneness as follows:

Medium-Rare - 125°F	Medium - 130°F
Medium-Well - 145°F	Well-Done - 150°F

Remove lamb chops from skillet and place on a warm plate.

Add shallots and sauté until softened. Add demi-glace, Worcestershire sauce, Dijon mustard, cherry preserves, marinated dried cherries, and stir. Simmer sauce until it reaches a sauce consistency.

Using a spoon, pull sauce back towards skillet handle, pull skillet back to heat the front of the skillet, pour Cherry Kirschwasser into front of skillet and heat 1 to 2 seconds, using a long match or wand lighter ignite Kirschwasser.

Once flame subsides, swirl in butter to finish sauce and drizzle sauce over lamb chops and serve.

Act III ~ Desserts

If Liquor, Liqueurs, and Sugar are a fault - then God help the Wicked!

Peaches Flambé

Bourbon Peach Flambé

Strawberries Romanoff

Bourbon Whiskey Apple Flambé

Brennan's Inspired Bananas Foster

Caribbean Bananas Flambé

Jamaican Bananas Flambé

Kathy's Apple & Banana Flambé

Crêpes Suzette

Cherries Jubilee

Act III ~ Desserts

Between the Sheets Flambé

Mango Flambé

Plantation Surprise

Pears with Rum Apricot Sauce

Pear Flambé

Crêpes D'Anjou

Flaming Baked Alaska's

Peaches Flambé: President Thomas Jefferson America's First Foodie!

President Thomas Jefferson is noted to be the first foodie in our country. He popularized ice cream, macarons, waffles, mac n cheese, tomatoes, and French fries in the United States. Along his journey he became a wine aficionado who consulted with several other Presidents on wine and what to serve to guests at the White House.

One of President Thomas Jefferson's favorite dishes to serve guests at his home, Monticello, was peaches flambé and ice cream. This was a very popular dish at Monticello, and the recipe for ice cream was written by Jefferson himself, on the back of his recipe for Savoy cookies. Jefferson loved peaches! To demonstrate his love of peaches, Jefferson had almost 900 peach trees of various varieties at Monticello that were used for a border around his property!

What's to be said, except, the introduction of Peaches Flambé by America's first foodie and his personal French trained chef, James Hemings, was a spectacular delight! I might debate you on what was more important, "The Declaration of Independence" or ice cream!

And for the trivia junkies, Presidents Thomas Jefferson and George Washington were our two largest purveyors of alcohol in the United States when they were alive - Samuel Adams eat your heart out.

Peaches Flambé is always a showstopper! Everyone always loves the cinnamon being sprinkled into the flame and getting a sparkler effect, and then the wonderful taste of the ingredients served over French Vanilla Ice Cream.

Enjoy!

Desserts

Peaches Flambé

*See "Supporting Cast" for French Vanilla Ice Cream recipe (page 176).

Serves 2

Ingredients

2 bowls French Vanilla Ice Cream*

1 can (1lb 13oz) Yellow Cling Peach Halves in Heavy Syrup

4 tablespoons butter

1/2 cup reserved peach heavy syrup

1/4 cup powdered sugar

Half an orange for zesting

1 whole orange, halved

4 reserved peach halves

1/2 ounce Triple Sec

1/2 ounce Cointreau

1/2 ounce Grand Marnier

1 ounce Don Q 151 Rum

1/2 teaspoon ground cinnamon

Directions

Scoop French Vanilla Ice Cream into bowls; freeze until firm and peaches are ready for serving.

Drain peaches and reserve 1/2 cup peach syrup in a decorative pitcher and 4 peach halves in a bowl.

Tableside Service:

Place a 12-inch skillet on a rechaud over medium flame heat, add and melt butter. Pour in reserved peach heavy syrup; bring to a bubble. Add powdered sugar and stir until sauce thickens slightly, about 3 to 5 minutes.

Zest an orange half over sauce. Squeeze juice from one half orange (if orange is on dry side, use both halves) over the sauce; cook an additional 2 to 3 minutes until mixture becomes syrupy and lightly coats a spoon. Add peach halves and heat peaches.

Using spoon, pull peaches back towards skillet handle, move skillet front over the heat, pour Triple Sec, Cointreau, Grand Marnier, and 151 Rum into front of skillet and heat 1 to 2 seconds, using a long match or wand lighter ignite the liquors. Sprinkle cinnamon into the flames to create flying embers. Stir liqueurs, rum and cinnamon into the sauce.

Serve over French Vanilla Ice Cream.

Bourbon Peach Flambé

Serves 2

Got Bourbon? Got peaches? Sounds like the beginning to a delicious concoction. Add butter and dark brown sugar and now you have a dynamite dessert! Though this is a very simple recipe with few ingredients, I think you are going to love it.

*See "Supporting Cast" for French Vanilla Ice Cream recipe (page 176).

Ingredients

2 bowls French Vanilla Ice Cream*

1 can (1lb 13oz) Yellow Cling Peach Halves in Heavy Syrup

2 tablespoons butter

2 tablespoons peach heavy syrup

1/4 cup dark brown sugar

4 reserved peach halves

2 ounces Bourbon Whiskey

1/2 teaspoon ground cinnamon

Directions

Scoop French Vanilla Ice Cream into bowls; freeze until firm and peaches are ready for serving.

Drain peaches and reserve 2 tablespoons peach heavy syrup in a decorative pitcher and place 4 peach halves in a bowl.

Tableside Service:

Place a 12-inch skillet on a rechaud over medium flame heat; add and melt the butter. Add the peach heavy syrup and brown sugar, stir until blended; reduce heat to medium low. Add peach halves and baste peaches with sauce, stirring occasionally, and turning peach halves gently with a spoon and fork.

Using a spoon, pull peaches back towards skillet handle, pull skillet back to heat front of skillet, pour Bourbon whiskey into front of skillet and heat 1 to 2 seconds, using a long match or wand lighter ignite the Bourbon whiskey. Sprinkle cinnamon into the flames to create flying embers. Stir Bourbon whiskey and cinnamon into the sauce.

Serve over French Vanilla Ice Cream and sprinkle with additional cinnamon.

Strawberries Romanoff

Serves 2

A version of Strawberries Romanoff was developed around the turn of the 20th century by the great chef Auguste Escoffier, when he was the chef at the Carlton Hotel in London. He called the recipe Strawberries Americaine Style. Fresh strawberries were marinated in fresh orange juice and Curacao Liqueur and topped with whipped cream.

In the 1940's or 1950's, the Hollywood restaurateur Mike Romanoff appropriated the recipe and had the dish on his menu. He called the dessert Strawberries Romanoff after the name of his restaurant. This version became a classic American dessert.

My version of Strawberries Romanoff is an elegant and very easy recipe to make and it tastes wonderful! The cinnamon is what makes this dessert recipe sparkle along with the other flavors.

*See "Supporting Cast" for Crème Fraîche recipe (page 179).

Ingredients

1/4 cup ultrafine granulated sugar

3 ounces Grand Marnier

2 cups fresh strawberries, rinsed, hulled, quartered

1 cup heavy whipping cream

2 tablespoons powdered sugar

1/3 cup Crème Fraîche* or sour cream

1/4 teaspoon ground cinnamon

Directions

In large bowl, combine the granulated sugar and 2 ounces Grand Marnier Liqueur; stir until the sugar dissolves. Add the berries and gently toss. Set aside to macerate 30 minutes. Dish up 1 cup berries into each of 2 large coupe glasses.

Whip the cream until foamy and gradually add the powdered sugar and remaining 1 ounce Grand Marnier. Beat until soft peaks form.

Tableside Service:

In a medium bowl, stir together whipped cream and the crème fraîche. Spoon cream mixture over the strawberries, garnish with a whole strawberry and sprinkle with cinnamon.

Bourbon Whiskey Apple Flambé

Serves 2

Some of my favorite things in life, cinnamon, butter, brown sugar and Bourbon! This recipe is featured in the section "Step by Step Flambé Directions".

*See "Supporting Cast" for French Vanilla Ice Cream recipe (page 176).

Ingredients

2 bowls French Vanilla Ice Cream*

2 Granny Smith apples, peeled, cored and cut in 1/4-inch slices

1 tablespoon lemon juice

4 tablespoons butter

4 tablespoons light brown sugar

2 ounces Bourbon Whiskey

1/2 teaspoon ground cinnamon

Directions

Scoop French Vanilla Ice Cream into bowls; freeze until firm and apples are ready for serving.

Combine the apple slices and lemon juice in a decorative bowl.

Tableside Service:

Place a 12-inch skillet on a rechaud over medium flame heat, melt butter. Add apples and cook, turning frequently, until crisp-tender, about 5 minutes. Stir in the brown sugar.

Using a spoon, pull apples back towards the skillet handle, pull skillet back to heat front of skillet, pour Bourbon whiskey into front of skillet and heat 1 to 2 seconds, using a long match or wand lighter ignite the Bourbon whiskey and stir sauce until the flames go out. Sprinkle cinnamon over the apples and stir into the sauce; spoon sauce over the apples.

Serve warm apples and sauce over French Vanilla Ice Cream. Garnish with a sprinkle of cinnamon.

Brennan's Inspired Bananas Foster

Serves 2

At the turn of the 20th century, big fruit companies were based in New Orleans, which was a major import center. Bananas were a major import into the Port of New Orleans and they were plentiful.

So, it's 1951, Ralph Brennan looked at his sister, who ran the restaurant Brennan's, and said, "come up with a new dessert for a dinner in honor of the new, New Orleans Crime Commission Chairman, Richard Foster". She chose a fruit that was plentiful, and with a low food cost, and the rest is history!

See "Supporting Cast" for French Vanilla Ice Cream recipe (page 176).

Ingredients

2 bowls of French Vanilla Ice Cream*

4 petite or 2 regular-sized bananas

4 tablespoons butter

1/3 cup packed light brown sugar

1/2 orange

1 ounce Cointreau

1 ounce 99 Bananas Liqueur

1 ounce Don Q 151 Rum

1/2 teaspoon ground cinnamon, *optional*

2 tablespoons chopped macadamia nuts

Directions

Scoop French Vanilla Ice Cream into bowls; freeze until firm and bananas are ready for serving.

Peel bananas, split in half lengthwise, and set on a decorative plate.

Tableside Service:

Place a 12-inch skillet on a rechaud over medium low heat; add and melt butter and stir in brown sugar until dissolved. Squeeze the orange over the skillet, stir juice into sauce. Add bananas to skillet and gently sauté 2 to 3 minutes.

Using a fork, gently pull bananas back towards skillet handle, pull skillet back to heat the front, pour Cointreau, 99 Bananas, and 151 Rum to front of skillet and heat front 1 to 2 seconds, using a long match or wand lighter ignite liquors, and, if using, sprinkle cinnamon into the flames. Stir liqueurs and rum into sauce and carefully spoon the sauce over the bananas, avoid breaking bananas.

Serve immediately over French Vanilla Ice Cream with a sprinkle of macadamia nuts.

Caribbean Bananas Flambé

Serves 2

With this dessert you'll feel the tropical island breezes, the sand between your toes, and the rhythm of the islands. So, you want a dessert with a hint of coconut and banana, followed by brown sugar and orange juice, well I have the perfect after dinner dessert for you.

*See "Supporting Cast" for French Vanilla Ice Cream recipe (page 176).

Ingredients

2 bowls French Vanilla Ice Cream*

1/4 cup whole pecans

4 petite or 2 regular-sized bananas

4 tablespoons butter

1/4 cup dark brown sugar

Juice of 1/2 orange

1 ounce 99 Bananas Liqueur

1 ounce Malibu Rum

1 ounce Meyers's Dark Rum

1/2 teaspoon ground cinnamon

1 tablespoon toasted sweetened shredded coconut

Directions

Scoop French Vanilla Ice Cream into bowls; freeze until firm and the bananas are ready to serve.

In a small skillet over medium heat, toast pecans until lightly browned, about 3 to 4 minutes.

Tableside Service:

In a 12-inch skillet on a rechaud over medium flame heat; add the butter, brown sugar, and stir. Once the sugar starts to dissolve, squeeze the orange over the skillet and stir juice into the sauce. Add bananas to the skillet and begin spooning the sauce over the bananas, flipping them after 1 minute.

Using your fork, gently move the bananas back towards skillet handle, pull skillet back to heat front of skillet, pour 99 Bananas Liqueur, Malibu Rum and Meyers's Rum into front skillet and heat 1 to 2 seconds, using a long match or wand lighter ignite the alcohols. Stir sauce until flames go out and gently spoon the sauce over the bananas.

Serve over French Vanilla Ice Cream and garnish with cinnamon, coconut and toasted pecans.

Jamaican Bananas Flambé

Serves 2

We wanted a new dessert using bananas besides Bananas Foster. So, we created this with flavors originating or grown in Jamaica. One of the popular spices in their culture and cooking is nutmeg. This spice pairs well with the dark, rich Myers's Dark Rum from Jamaica. To add more flavor from the Caribbean we used dark brown sugar which originated in the Caribbean during the 1700's. Finally, we chose cashews to top off the dessert as cashews are a native nut tree in Jamaica. Kathy and I hope you enjoy this history lesson as much as the dessert.

*See "Supporting Cast" for French Vanilla Ice Cream recipe (page 176).

Ingredients

2 bowls French Vanilla Ice Cream*

4 petite or 2 regular-sized bananas

4 tablespoons butter

1/3 cup dark brown sugar

1/2 large orange

1/2 teaspoon freshly ground nutmeg

2 ounces Myers's Dark Rum

2 tablespoons chopped roasted, salted cashews

Directions

Scoop French Vanilla Ice Cream into bowls; freeze until firm and bananas are ready for serving.

Peel bananas, slice on a diagonal into 2-inch chunks and set on decorative plate.

Tableside Service:

Place a 12-inch skillet on a rechaud over medium low heat; add and melt butter then stir in brown sugar until dissolved. Squeeze the orange over the skillet, add nutmeg, and stir juice and nutmeg into the sauce. Add bananas to skillet and gently sauté 2 to 3 minutes, turning once.

Using a fork, gently pull bananas back towards skillet handle, pull skillet back to heat front, pour Myers's Dark Rum into front of skillet and heat front 1 to 2 seconds, using a long match or wand lighter ignite rum. As the flames go out, stir the rum into the sauce. Carefully spoon the sauce over the bananas, avoid breaking bananas.

Spoon bananas and sauce over ice cream and sprinkle with chopped cashews. A dash of nutmeg over the top to finish the dessert.

Kathy's Apple & Banana Flambé

Serves 2

My wife was visiting Spokane, Washington on business and went to the Davenport Hotel for dinner and to see my twin brother who was working there in the dining room. When she was finished with dinner, she asked my twin what he recommended for dessert and the following recipe is what they made for her.

*See "Supporting Cast" for French Vanilla Ice Cream recipe (page 176).

Ingredients

2 bowls French Vanilla Ice Cream*

1 Granny Smith apple peeled, cored and sliced

1 banana, sliced in half lengthwise

4 tablespoons butter

1/2 cup light brown sugar

1/2 ounce Bacardi White Rum

1 ounce Calvados Apple Brandy

1/2 ounce Grand Marnier

1/2 teaspoon ground cinnamon

Directions

Scoop French Vanilla Ice Cream into bowls; freeze until firm and apple and bananas are ready for serving.

Arrange apple slices and banana halves on a decorative plate.

Tableside Service:

Place a 12-inch skillet on a rechaud over medium heat; add and melt butter, stir in brown sugar until dissolved. Add apples and sauté for 2 minutes, add bananas to skillet and gently sauté both for 2 to 3 minutes until bananas are easily pierced with a fork. Carefully spoon the sauce over the apples and bananas, avoid breaking both fruits.

Using a fork gently pull apples and bananas back towards skillet handle, pull skillet back to heat the front of the skillet, pour in Bacardi White Rum, Calvados, and Grand Marnier to front of skillet and heat 1 to 2 seconds, using a long match or wand lighter ignite liquors and liqueur and stir until flame goes out. Sprinkle cinnamon over sauce and stir into the sauce.

Spoon apples, bananas and sauce over French Vanilla Ice Cream.

Crêpes Suzette

Serves 2

One of Kathy's and my favorite artists is Guy Buffet, French painter and illustrator, as we appreciate his paintings of characters in restaurants, chefs, sommeliers, waiters and bartenders. Each time I see one of his paintings, I reminisce about my time as a Flambé Chef and working in restaurants. Kathy discovered that Guy Buffet had painted an original watercolor entitled "Crêpes Suzette". In appreciation of my background, Kathy gave me the painting for my birthday and it was the perfect birthday gift. Kathy approached the art gallery and asked them if Mr. Buffet would write a dedication in exchange for a copy of our cookbook French Flambé Cooking at Home...and he agreed and sent me a card with a note.

The provenance of Crêpes Suzette is disputed. One account is Henri Charpentier, a young waiter at the Maître at Monte Carlo's Café de Paris, serendipitously invented the recipe while working in front of a chafing dish preparing crêpes for the Prince of Wales, the future King Edward VII, and the cordials caught fire. Charpentier thought the dish ruined but still served it and it was a success. When asked for the name of the dessert, Charpentier called the dessert Crêpes Princesse. The prince, then requested that the dessert be named for a young woman in attendance, Suzette.

When people talk to me about which dessert recipe is my favorite, I have to say Crêpes Suzette! Where Peaches Flambé is the prettiest to watch be made, to me Crêpes Suzette is the one that tastes the best!

*See "Supporting Cast" for Crêpes (page 182) and Heavy Simple Syrup (page 180) recipes.

Ingredients

6 Crêpes*, folded in half, folded in half again

8 tablespoons butter

1/4 cup Heavy Simple Syrup*

Zest of 1/2 orange

1/2 juicy orange

2/3 cup powdered sugar

1 ounce Cointreau

1 ounce Grand Marnier

1/2 ounce Don Q 151 Rum

Powdered sugar for garnish

Directions

Prepare crêpes and set on a decorative plate.

Tableside Service:

Place a 12-inch skillet on a rechaud over medium flame heat; add butter and melt, pour in heavy syrup. Zest orange half over sauce, squeeze orange over skillet and stir zest and juice into sauce. Add the powdered sugar; stir until sauce thickens and coats the spoon.

Add crêpes to skillet, spoon sauce over crêpes. Gently move crêpes back toward skillet handle, pull skillet back to heat front of skillet, pour Cointreau, Grand Marnier and 151 Rum into front of skillet and heat 1 to 2 seconds, using a long match or lighter ignite liqueurs and rum, stir sauce until flames go out.

Dish 3 crêpes onto 2 plates. Spoon sauce and sift powdered sugar lightly over the crêpes and serve.

To David.

Crepes suzette is an homage to one facet of your life as a flambé Chef and for being the flame in your wife's heart

Original Watercolor "Crêpes Suzette" Dedication by Artist Guy Buffet

Cherries Jubilee

Serves 2

Cherries Jubilee is a popular dessert with little known history. Its creation is credited to Auguste Escoffier, who created it for Queen Victoria. Based on her love of cherries, Escoffier prepared the dish as a tribute to Queen Victoria for her Diamond Jubilee celebration in 1897. These Jubilees were essentially anniversaries, celebrating the number of years Victoria had ruled. Depending upon which account you credit, the invention of Cherries Jubilee could be dated to either 1887, the Queen's 50th year of rule, or 1897, Victoria's 60th anniversary as Queen.

I know other desserts are more impressive to watch be made, but this dessert ranks in the very top of desserts. The dark cherries in a glistening Schladerer Cherry Kirschwasser sauce served over French Vanilla Ice Cream is as good as it gets as far as I'm concerned. Enjoy!

*See "Supporting Cast" for French Vanilla Ice Cream recipe (page 176).

Ingredients

2 bowls French Vanilla Ice Cream*

1 can (15 ounces) Oregon Specialty Fruit Dark Sweet Cherries in Heavy Syrup

1 cup powdered sugar

1 ounce Schladerer Cherry Kirschwasser

1 ounce Cointreau

1 ounce Don Q 151 Rum

Directions

Scoop French Vanilla Ice Cream into bowls; freeze until firm and cherries are ready for serving.

Drain cherries, reserving juice and place cherries in a presentation bowl and cherry heavy syrup in a pitcher.

Tableside Service:

Place a 12-inch skillet on a rechaud over medium flame heat, pour cherry juice into skillet. Stir in 3/4 of the powdered sugar, bring to a gentle boil, and cook sauce until syrupy and coats a spoon, 2 to 3 minutes. If sauce is too thin, add remaining sugar and gently boil 2 to 3 more minutes. Add cherries and heat 1 to 2 minutes.

Using a spoon, pull cherries back towards skillet handle, pull skillet back to heat front, pour Kirschwasser, Cointreau, and 151 Rum into front of skillet and heat front 1 to 2 seconds, using a long match or wand lighter light liquors and liqueur, and stir liquors and liqueur into sauce until flames go out.

Serve cherries and sauce over French Vanilla Ice Cream.

Between the Sheets Flambé

Serves 2

Remember, when I told you my family was French, and we came to this country through the Port of New Orleans. Now, imagine you are seated with me in the French Quarter having this dessert with the aromas, sounds, and the tastes of old New Orleans.

This dessert is a spin-off of the cocktails Between the Sheets and Sidecar both popular in the 1850's New Orleans.

*See "Supporting Cast" for French Vanilla Ice Cream recipe (page 176).

Ingredients

2 bowls French Vanilla Ice Cream*

4 tablespoons butter

1/4 cup granulated sugar

1 orange

1/2 lemon

4 slices fresh pineapple rings

1 ounce VSOP Cognac

1 ounce Meyers's Dark Rum

1 ounce Malibu Rum

Directions

Scoop French Vanilla Ice Cream onto a plate or tray; freeze until firm and pineapple slices are ready for serving.

Tableside Service:

Place 12-inch skillet on a rechaud over medium flame heat; add butter and melt. Add sugar and stir until sugar is melted. Squeeze the orange and lemon over skillet, stir the orange and lemon juices into the sauce. Allow sauce to simmer until slightly syrupy. Spread pineapple slices in the skillet and cook 2 to 3 minutes basting with sauce.

Using a fork, gently pull rings back towards skillet handle, pull skillet back to heat skillet front, pour Cognac and rums into the front of skillet and heat 1 to 2 seconds, using a long match or wand lighter light Cognac and rums. As flames go out, stir Cognac and rums into sauce.

To serve, place a pineapple ring on a plate, top with a scoop or scoops of French Vanilla Ice Cream, place another pineapple ring on the side of the ice cream, and spoon sauce over top.

Mango Flambé

Serves 2

We have a Family Dinner Party once or twice a year. We always try to serve something new and different. We developed this recipe for one of these dinners as mango was fresh and plentiful. One of our family members, Shelley Simas, wanted to learn how to flambé so I had Shelley help me prepare this dessert dish and learn how to flambé.

*See "Supporting Cast" for French Vanilla Ice Cream recipe (page 176).

Ingredients

2 bowls French Vanilla Ice Cream*

4 tablespoons butter

1/2 cup light brown sugar

2 ripe mangos, peeled, diced in bite-sized chunks

1 ounce Grand Marnier

2 ounces Meyers's Dark Rum

1/2 teaspoon ground cinnamon

Directions

Scoop French Vanilla Ice Cream into bowls; freeze until firm and mango chunks are ready for serving.

Tableside Service:

In a 12-inch skillet on a rechaud over medium flame heat, add butter and melt. Add brown sugar and heat until sugar melts; add mango chunks and cook 3 to 4 minutes.

Using a spoon, pull mango chunks back towards skillet handle, pull skillet back to heat front of skillet, pour Grand Marnier and Meyers's Rum into front of skillet and heat 1 to 2 seconds, and using a long match or wand lighter ignite the liqueur and rums. Sprinkle cinnamon into the flames. Stir liqueur and rum and cinnamon into the sauce.

Serve over French Vanilla Ice Cream.

Plantation Surprise

Serves 2

If you have a Hawaiian or an Asian themed dinner party, this dessert has delicious exotic fruits and flavors. Using the pineapple shell as the boat for the dessert filled with the fruit's vibrant colors of green, oranges, and yellows is a showstopper. The homemade orange sherbet topping slowly melts and combines with the fruit and sauce taking this dessert to a culinary experience. This dessert takes a little more effort, but I think you will find that it is well worth it!

*See "Supporting Cast" for Heavy Simple Syrup (page 180) and Orange Sherbet recipes (page 181).

Ingredients

1 fresh, small pineapple

1/2 cup fresh papaya cubes

1/2 cup fresh mango cubes

2 kiwis, peeled, sliced

1 medium banana, peeled, sliced

4 tablespoons butter

1/2 cup Heavy Simple Syrup*

1/2 ounce Cointreau

1/2 ounce Grand Marnier

1 ounce Don Q 151 Rum

2 large scoops Orange Sherbet*

Flaked sweetened coconut

Macadamia nuts, coarsely chopped

Directions

To create a pineapple boat, cut pineapple in half lengthwise through the leaf top to the bottom. Carefully remove pineapple from shell. Remove pineapple core and cut pineapple into bite-sized chunks.

Gently toss together 1 cup pineapple chunks with papaya, mango, kiwi, and banana, place in decorative bowl.

Tableside Service:

Place a 12-inch skillet on a rechaud over medium flame heat, melt butter together with simple syrup. Add tropical fruit, stir to coat fruit and simmer 1 to 2 minutes.

Pull fruit back towards skillet handle, pull skillet back to heat front of skillet, pour in Cointreau, Grand Marnier and 151 Rum to front of skillet and heat 1 to 2 seconds, using a long match or wand lighter ignite the liqueurs and rum. As the flames go out, stir liqueurs and rum into sauce and fruit.

Spoon fruit into pineapple boats, top with a scoop of orange sherbet and sprinkle with coconut and macadamia nuts.

Pears with Rum Apricot Sauce

Serves 2

I grew up in the Pacific Northwest and discovered hazelnuts as a child. Their flavor can be described as nutty, toasty, and earthy. The hazelnuts are a perfect complement for the tender pears and smooth apricot sauce providing a crunchy texture. The vanilla extract with the Frangelico then gives the recipe a hazelnut custard taste with the pear.

See "Supporting Cast" for the recipe for French Vanilla Ice Cream (page 176).

Ingredients

2 bowls French Vanilla Ice Cream*

2 D' Anjou pears, ripened

2 cups cold water

1/4 cup honey

6 tablespoons butter

1/2 cup powdered sugar

1/2 cup apricot preserves

1/2 teaspoon vanilla extract

1 ounce Frangelico Liqueur

2 ounces Bacardi White Rum

2 tablespoons toasted, chopped hazelnuts

Directions

Scoop French Vanilla Ice Cream into bowls or on to a plate; freeze until firm and pear halves are ready for serving.

Peel, halve and core pears; mix honey into water and add pears to soak for 5 minutes. Drain pears and place on a decorative plate.

Tableside Service:

Place a 12-inch skillet on a rechaud over flame medium heat, melt butter and stir in powdered sugar. Stir in apricot preserves; add pears to the sauce and simmer gently, basting the pears with the sauce, until the pears have just turned tender, about 2 to 3 minutes. Stir vanilla extract into the sauce.

Gently pull pears back towards skillet handle, pull the skillet back to heat the front, pour Frangelico and Bacardi White Rum to the front of the skillet and heat 1 to 2 seconds, using a long match or a wand lighter light the liqueur and rum, when the flames go out stir liqueur and rum into the sauce.

Gently lift pears from the pan and put on ice cream and spoon sauce over the top. Sprinkle with hazelnuts and serve.

Pear Flambé

Serves 2

This is a very easy dessert to make even for someone of very little skill in the kitchen. Five ingredients combine to make a lite dessert with the pear being the star of the show. Then the rum gives the recipe a richness and the cinnamon joins the party at the end to give the recipe a nice finish with a little pizazz!

*See "Supporting Cast" for French Vanilla Ice Cream recipe (page 176).

Ingredients

2 bowls French Vanilla Ice Cream*

2 D' Anjou Pears

2 cups water

1/4 cup honey

4 tablespoons butter

1/2 cup powdered sugar

2 tablespoons pear poaching liquid

2 ounces Myers's Dark Rum

1/2 ounce Don Q 151 Rum

1/2 teaspoon ground cinnamon

Directions

Scoop French Vanilla Ice Cream into bowls; freeze until firm and pear halves are ready for serving.

Heat water with the honey until simmering. Peel, halve and core pears; add pears to poaching liquid and poach 10 minutes. Reserve 2 tablespoons pear poaching liquid; drain pears and place on a decorative plate.

Tableside Service:

Place a 12-inch skillet on a rechaud over medium flame heat; add and melt butter. Stir in sugar and pear poaching liquid; when the sugar has melted, add pear halves and cook 3 to 4 minutes spooning sauce over the pears.

Gently pull pears back towards skillet handle, pull skillet back to heat the front of the skillet, pour the Meyers's Dark Rum and 151 Rum into front of skillet and heat 1 to 2 seconds, using a long match or wand lighter ignite the rums, as flames go out stir rums into the sauce.

Spoon pears and sauce over French Vanilla Ice Cream and serve.

Crêpes D' Anjou

Serves 2

My niece Michele came to visit us from Washington DC. She is the definition of a "foodie", so we wanted to create something new that she hadn't experienced. We knew we had been successful when my niece called and requested the recipe.

*See "Supporting Cast" for Crêpes (page 182), Chocolate Ganache Sauce (page 183), and French Vanilla Ice Cream (page 176) recipes.

Ingredients

1 pear, peeled, cored, sliced lengthwise

1 cup water

2 tablespoons honey

4 tablespoons butter

1/4 cup powdered sugar

2 ounces Williams Pear Brandy

2 Crêpes*

1/2 cup Chocolate Ganache Sauce*

4 scoops, 2 ounces each, French Vanilla Ice Cream*

Directions

Place pear slices in a bowl with water and honey; soak 5 minutes, drain and place in a decorative bowl.

Tableside Service:

Place a 12-inch skillet on a rechaud over medium flame heat; add butter and melt, add sugar. Stirring constantly, cook until sugar begins to melt. Add pear slices and gently stir to cook pears, about 2 to 3 minutes.

Pull pear slices back towards skillet handle, pull skillet back to heat the front of the skillet, pour in the William Pear Brandy into front of skillet and heat 1 to 2 seconds, light pear brandy with a long match or wand lighter. As flames go out, stir pear brandy into the sauce.

On 2 dessert plates: place a crêpe on each plate, drizzle 1/4 cup chocolate ganache sauce down center of the crêpe, place 2 small scoops of ice cream on top of sauce, fold crêpe leaves over ice cream.

Top crêpes with sautéed pears, pear brandy sauce and a drizzle of chocolate ganache sauce.

Baked Alaska

I'm including the whole story about Baked Alaska, because it is one of the oldest flamed recipes. Also, this recipe was a very big deal at the time it was originated. Ice cream and bananas were not readily available in that time period and a meal at Delmonico's restaurant would cost most people one month's salary. So, only the very wealthy ate at this restaurant. Hope you enjoyed the history lesson. The article below is the history of this dish and how it came to be and is not my work, but I trust it's accuracy.

History of Baked Alaska

"Like most culinary innovations, baked Alaska didn't exactly appear out of the blue. The concept of serving ice cream into a warm casing had already been explored. For instance, Thomas Jefferson is thought to have served ice cream encased in a hot pastry at a White House state banquet in 1802, the second year of his presidency (Incidentally, that banquet is also thought to have provided the moment Jefferson introduced the newly formed United States to what would go on to become another of its signature dishes: Mac 'n' Cheese. Like the baked Alaska ancestor, that too was served as more of a pie).

How the baked Alaska specifically – cake topped with ice cream covered in meringue – was born is still debated, but it's thought to have begun with the work of an American-born scientist called Sir Benjamin Thompson.

Thompson served as a spy and informant for the British Army during the American Revolution. When the war ended in 1776, he was forced to flee to England and, later, Bavaria, where he was made a Count of the Holy Roman Empire. He took the name Count Rumford, after Rumford (now Concord), New Hampshire, where he was married.

Count Rumford was also a physicist and inventor with a keen interest in heat management. He invented thermal underwear, among many other things, and revolutionized the design of the chimney to extract smoke more efficiently.

But just as importantly, Rumford's fascination with heat spilled over into cooking. He's credited with inventing the sous vide technique and, just a couple of years after Jefferson served ice cream pie at the White House (and perhaps inspired by the idea), he also discovered something incredible about meringue.

Meringue, as a consequence of all the air bubbles trapped inside, is a poor conductor of heat and makes for a great insulator. In fact, it's an effective enough insulator to momentarily slow the melting of ice cream under an intense heat.

That's where things get hazy. What we do know is that the Omelette Norwegge somehow migrated back to Count Rumford's homeland and, once stateside, became the baked Alaska.

The best guess is that Charles Ranhofer, a Parisian pastry chef working at New York's famous Delmonico's restaurant, introduced it circa 1867, either to celebrate or to poke fun at New York senator William H. Seward's purchase of Alaska from the Russians, which was widely ridiculed at the time. Ranhofer called his dessert 'Alaska, Florida', to reference the combination of cold and hot components. It consisted of banana ice cream on a walnut spice cake, with the exterior meringue torched golden brown – just as it's still served at Delmonico's today.

However, evidence to suggest that Ranhofer got in there first with the Alaska reference is flaky. Sure, it's the strongest link to an origin story we have, but we can't rule out the possibility that chefs in North America simply adapted the Omelette Norwegge moniker to instead reference their own snowy region to the north.

Of course, we couldn't wrap up an article on baked Alaska without sharing with you how to actually make one."

-By Fine Dining Lovers, 28 JUL 2021

Flaming Baked Alaska's

Serves 6

In 1867, Charles Ranhofer, the French chef at New York's famous Delmonico's restaurant created a new cake to commemorate the purchase of Alaska from the Russians and called it "Alaska, Florida". This dessert became what we know today as "Baked Alaska".

Baked Alaska is an old-fashioned dessert of cake and ice cream swathed in meringue. It looks impressive to light the dessert on fire. If you have never tried it, you should try it at least once. I made slight changes to Delmonico's original recipe and changed the ingredient amounts to serve 4 or 6.

*See "Supporting Cast" for Banana Ice Cream (page 184), French Walnut Sponge Cake (page 187), Apricot Compote (page 188) and Swiss Meringue (page 189) recipes.

Ingredients

6 1/2-cup scoops Banana Ice Cream*

6 3-inch round French Walnut Sponge Cakes*

3/4 cup Apricot Compote*

1 batch Swiss Meringue*

3 ounces or 1/2 ounce Don Q 151 Rum per individual Baked Alaska cake

Directions

Scoop 6 scoops of banana ice cream onto small cookie sheet, freeze until hardened.

Place cakes on a cookie sheet, top each cake with 1 tablespoon apricot compote, and freeze 10 minutes. Place frozen scoops of banana ice cream on top of each cake. Freeze cake and ice cream until Swiss Meringue is ready.

Place each cake on a heatproof plate. Using a pastry bag and Wilton 1M tip, pipe meringue to completely cover the cake and ice cream or use a knife to cover. Using a kitchen torch, brown meringue.

Tableside Service:

In a small saucepan, heat 151 Rum, ignite with long match or wand lighter and drizzle rum over Baked Alaska cakes and serve flaming cakes.

Encore

Your guests will applaud your culinary efforts and will call "encore, encore!" when an after dinner coffee is offered....

Spanish Coffee

Irish Coffee

Café Brûlot Diabolique

Café Royale

Spanish Coffee

Serves 1

The Corajillo is a hot coffee drink with origins in the Spain and Latin countries and may be made with rum, mezcal or coffee liqueur. The Fernwood Inn, in Milwaukie, Oregon, stole the recipe from a bar in Mexico and started the drink. Then James Louie from Huber's Restaurant stole it and did his own version by making the drink tableside. Huber's drink starts with the lighting of 151 Rum, swirling the glass to allow the flames to caramelize the glass's sugar rim, then adding Kahlua, Triple Sec, hot coffee and topped with a blanket of cream...this became Huber's Spanish Coffee and the tableside preparation is truly impressive.

One night in the Rodeway Inn's dining room Darrell and I had a request to make two Spanish Coffees. No big deal, we had done it hundreds of times. Well, we were finishing up on the table when things got exciting. It started when we were closing the lid on the liquid sterno and we accidently spilled it into the middle of the dining table we were working at. OMG, we had a fire on a table in the middle of a packed dining room. Darrell and I were scrambling to find and grab water glasses from surrounding tables to put out the mini bonfire. Finally, the fire was out and the linen for the table was changed and the two little old ladies were able to enjoy their Spanish Coffees in peace and quiet.

Our Spanish Coffee story would end there, but twenty minutes went by and the waiter for the table said, "The ladies at the table wanted to see you and Darrell again". Darrell and I couldn't imagine what they wanted other than to chew us out. We arrived at the table and the ladies started with, "We want to thank you for one of the most exciting evenings of our lives. A wonderful meal, drama, then a great coffee drink. It is the most fun we have had in years!", then they asked for two more Spanish Coffee's!

*See "Supporting Cast" for Whipped Cream recipe (page 190).

Ingredients

1 lemon wedge, split in middle

1/4 cup granulated sugar

1 ounce Old Bushmills Black Bush Irish Whiskey

1/2 ounce Tia Maria

4 ounces freshly brewed black coffee, regular or decaffeinated

1/2 cup Whipped Cream*

1/2 ounce Kahlua

Directions

Tableside Service:

Using the lemon wedge, place split over the rim of a heat tempered mug or glass; rub split around the rim of the mug or glass. Dip the wet rim of the mug or glass into a bowl filled with the granulated sugar to coat.

Gently warm Irish whiskey. Pour the Irish whiskey into the mug or glass. With a long match or wand lighter, carefully light the whiskey and swirl the whiskey in the mug or glass to melt the sugar on the rim. Put out flame with the coffee, pour in Tia Maria, and top with the whipped cream. Drizzle Kahlua over the top of the whipped cream. Serve immediately.

Alternatively: Using a crème brûlée torch, heat the sugar around the rim of the mug or glass until it starts to caramelize and turn brown.

Irish Coffee

Serves 1

Irish Coffee was created in the winter of 1943 by Joe Sheridan, chef at Foynes Port near Limerick, Ireland.

Sheridan was the head chef at the restaurant and coffee shop in the Foynes Airbase. One evening a flight headed for New York returned to Foynes after battling rough weather for several hours. Chef Sheridan, feeling empathy for the delayed, cold and weary passengers, decided to whip up something special for them to drink and the Irish Coffee was born.

My recipe for Irish Coffee has a few more ingredients than just Irish whiskey. It also brings back fond memories of being at the Rodeway Inn on a cold and rainy night and needing something warm after a shift. I had forgotten how wonderful this version is until I remade this for the cookbook, I want to emphasize to use real whipped cream. IT MAKES THE DRINK!

*See "Supporting Cast" for Whipped Cream recipe (page 190).

Ingredients

Lemon wedge, split in middle

1/4 cup granulated sugar

1 teaspoon sugar

2 ounces Old Bushmill Black Bush Irish Whiskey

1/2 ounce Kahlua

4 ounces freshly brewed hot coffee, regular or decaffeinated

1/2 cup Whipped Cream*

Chocolate covered coffee beans

Directions

In a butter warmer or small saucepan over low heat, heat the Old Bushmills to a simmer with gentle bubbles around edge; remove from heat.

Tableside Service:

Using a lemon wedge, place the split over the rim of a heat tempered mug or glass; rub split around the rim. Dip the wet rim of the mug or glass into a bowl filled with granulated sugar to coat.

Place teaspoon of sugar into the mug or glass and pour the warm Old Bushmills into the mug or glass. With a long match or wand lighter, carefully light the whiskey and swirl the whiskey in the mug or glass to melt the sugar on the rim. Put out the flame with Kahlua then pour in the coffee.

Top with a large dollop of whipped cream and a chocolate covered coffee bean.

Serve immediately

Café Brûlot Diabolique

Serves 2

I watched Walide Saleeby, Rodeway Inn Maître 'D and Flame Captain, prepare this coffee. Café Brûlot Diabolique was hypnotic to watch being prepared. Cointreau and Cognac were poured into a chafing dish to warm and then lit on fire. Using the French fork and spoon service to hold a spiralized orange peel studded with whole cloves over the chafing dish, a ladle was used to drizzle the flaming alcohol over the spiral orange peel spiraling down into the alcohol with the essence of orange and cloves. Once two to three ladles was drizzled over the orange peel, coffee was added into the chafing dish. The coffee was ladled into cups and served.

Café Brûlot Diabolique, or "Devilishly Burned Coffee," was invented at Antoine's Restaurant in the late 1880s by Jules Alciatore, the son of the restaurant's founder. According to Phillip Collier's Mixing New Orleans, Alciatore was inspired by French bon vivants who would drown a sugar cube in Cognac and place it over an open flame before extinguishing it in a cup of hot coffee. Today, you can still find the drink in New Orleans at restaurants including Antoine's, Galatoire's and Arnaud's.

Our version is easier and safer but, retains the dramatic effect and flavor of the original recipe.

*See "Supporting Cast" for Whipped Cream recipe (page 190)

Ingredients

1 orange

10 whole cloves

1 lemon

3 tablespoons granulated sugar

2 cups freshly brewed black coffee, regular or decaffeinated

2 cinnamon sticks

1 ounce Cointreau

2 ounces VSOP Cognac

1/2 cup Whipped Cream*

1 ounce Grand Marnier

Directions

Spiral peel the orange; along the length of the peel pierce the peel with the whole cloves. Spiral peel the lemon.

Tableside Service:

Place a 2-quart saucepan on a rechaud over medium-high heat. Add into the saucepan the sugar, coffee, orange and lemon peels and cinnamon sticks; simmer to infuse the coffee with the citrus and spices, about 5 to 7 minutes.

In a small stainless saucepan over low heat, warm the Cointreau and Cognac. When the coffee is ready, using a long match or wand lighter light the alcohol. Starting right above the coffee, pour the alcohol into the coffee and raise up the saucepan while pouring for dramatic effect. Stir the alcohol into the spiced coffee. Swirl the coffee until the flames go out.

Ladle the coffee into brûlot or demitasse cups. Garnish with a dollop of whipped cream, add a cinnamon stick, and then a drizzle of Grand Marnier, serve.

Café Royale

Serves 1

This was not a flaming coffee at the Eugene Hotel, but it is one we prepared tableside for our customers. The twist with the caramel sauce created a sweet and buttery after dinner coffee. To change this to a flaming coffee, I heated the Cognac in a saucepan, or a chafing dish, and lit the Cognac. I then added the coffee and caramel sauce topped it with whipped cream which merged to create a rich, smooth after dinner coffee.

*See "Supporting Cast" for Whipped Cream recipe (page 190).

Ingredients

2 ounces VSOP Cognac

4 ounces freshly brewed hot coffee, regular or decaffeinated

2 tablespoons Torani caramel sauce

1/2 cup Whipped Cream*

Unsweetened cocoa powder

Directions

Tableside Service:

Place a 1-quart saucepan on a rechaud over medium-high flame; pour in the VSOP Cognac, heat about 10 seconds, then using a long match or wand lighter carefully ignite the Cognac.

Allow Cognac to flame 4 to 5 seconds then pour in coffee and stir in caramel sauce until the sauce is dissolved. Pour mixture into a 12-ounce coffee mug and top with a couple of large dollops of whipped cream.

To finish the drink, sprinkle cocoa over the top and serve.

Supporting Cast

Behind every great performance there is a cast of characters who support the star. Think of the asparagus without the hollandaise or the tenderloin without the béarnaise; while each one is great on their own, they are even more delicious together.

The recipes to follow are those characters whose flavors enhance the performance of the star in a recipe.

Caeser Croutons

Yogurt Sauce

Peach Chutney

Sweet & Spicy Candied Pecans

Thermidor Lobster Stock

Thermidor Mushrooms

Lobster Thermidor Sauce

Mango Chutney

Orange Sauce

Supporting Cast

Dark Sweet Cherry Sauce

Bordelaise Red Wine Sauce

Champignon Sauce

Chasseur Sauce

Roasted Beef Tenderloin

Roasted Tomato Crowns

Duchess Potatoes

Béarnaise Sauce

French Vanilla Ice Cream

Crème Fraîche

Heavy Simple Syrup

Supporting Cast

Continued

Orange Sherbet

Crêpes

Chocolate Ganache

Banana Ice Cream

French Walnut Sponge Cake

Apricot Compote

Swiss Meringue

Whipped Cream

Caeser Croutons

Ingredient

2 tablespoons extra-virgin olive oil

1/4 teaspoon kosher salt

2 cups day old rustic Italian bread, crusts removed, cut in 1/2 inch cubes

Directions

Preheat oven to 350°F.

In a large bowl mix together the olive oil, melted butter, and salt. Add bread cubes to the bowl, toss until coated. Spread the bread cubes out in a single layer on a baking sheet. Bake for about 15 to 20 minutes, or until golden brown and very dry. About halfway through, stir once to brown evenly. Cool, store in an airtight container.

Yogurt Sauce

For this sauce, Kathy prefers to use Fage® Greek yogurt. It has a mild acidic tang and is very creamy which is perfect for yogurt sauces.

Ingredients

1 1/2 cups plain whole-milk Greek yogurt

1/2 English cucumber, peeled, shredded and squeezed dry

1 tablespoon fresh lemon juice

2 garlic, cloves, finely grated

2 tablespoons coarsely chopped fresh dill

Kosher salt and freshly ground black pepper

Directions

Mix all ingredients together and chill.

Peach Chutney

Ingredients

1 cup chopped fresh, peeled and pitted peaches or frozen peaches, thawed, drained

1 teaspoon lime juice

2 tablespoons granulated sugar

2 tablespoons apple cider vinegar

1 tablespoon golden raisins

1 tablespoon currants

1/2 teaspoon finely minced fresh ginger

1 small clove garlic, finely minced

2 teaspoons minced shallot

1/4 teaspoon kosher salt

1/8 teaspoon crushed red pepper flakes

1/8 teaspoon ground cinnamon

Directions

Toss peaches and lime juice together, set aside.

In a small saucepan, mix sugar, vinegar, raisins, currants, ginger, garlic, shallot, salt, red pepper flakes and cinnamon. Add peaches and bring to a boil. Reduce heat and simmer for 10 minutes until chutney reaches a jam-like consistency.

Will keep in the refrigerator for several days.

Sweet & Spicy Candied Pecans

These pecans are delicious as a cocktail snack or as a topping for salads.

Ingredients

1/2 cup pecan halves

1 tablespoon granulated sugar

1 1/2 teaspoons water

1/8 teaspoon freshly ground black pepper

1/8 teaspoon cayenne pepper

Kosher salt

Directions

Line a baking sheet with parchment paper and set aside.

Place a non-stick skillet over medium heat. Pour the pecan halves into the dry skillet and toast them 3 to 4 minutes or until pecans become fragrant.

Add the sugar, water, cayenne and black pepper to the skillet. The sugar will melt into the water almost immediately, creating a syrup. Using a spatula stir pecans to make sure the pecans are evenly covered in syrup. Turn off the heat.

Pour the glazed pecans across the parchment paper lined baking sheet and sprinkle them with a pinch of salt. Allow the pecans to fully cool at room temperature.

Thermidor Lobster Stock

This stock recipe has a rich lobster flavor and can be used for Lobster Bisque.

Ingredients

1 cup dry white wine

1/3 cup chopped onion

1/3 cup chopped carrot

1/3 cup chopped celery

4 sprigs fresh Italian parsley

1 bay leaf

1 sprig thyme

1 teaspoon dried tarragon

4 lobster tail shells, chopped into 2-inch pieces

2 cups water

Directions

In a 3-quart saucepan, bring stock ingredients to a boil then reduce and simmer for 1 hour. Strain then, if necessary, boil down stock until liquid has reduced to 1 1/2 cups.

Reserve 3/4 cup stock for Lobster Thermidor Sauce, freeze remaining stock.

Thermidor Mushrooms

Ingredients

1/2 pound fresh mushrooms, cleaned, trimmed, quartered

3 tablespoons water

1 tablespoon butter

1 teaspoon lemon juice

1/4 teaspoon kosher salt

Directions

Place mushrooms in a 1-quart saucepan with water, butter, lemon juice, and salt. Cover saucepan and simmer 10 minutes.

Strain mushroom liquid and reserve 1/4 cup for Lobster Thermidor Sauce. Set mushrooms aside for Lobster Thermidor.

Lobster Thermidor Sauce

Ingredients

2 tablespoons butter

2 tablespoons all-purpose flour

3/4 cup lobster stock

1/4 cup Thermidor Mushrooms stock

1/4 cup heavy whipping cream

1 egg yolk

1 teaspoon dry mustard

1/8 teaspoon dried tarragon

1/4 teaspoon kosher salt

Pinch cayenne pepper

Directions

Melt butter in 3-quart saucepan, stir in flour and cook slowly, about 2 minutes. Slowly pour in lobster and mushroom stocks, stir vigorously with a wire whip. Bring to a boil, stirring about 1 minute. Remove from heat.

In large bowl, beat together heavy cream, egg yolk, dry mustard, tarragon, salt, and cayenne pepper. Temper egg yolk by slowly beating in half of the hot sauce. Pour egg yolk mixture into the hot sauce.

Set sauce over medium heat; stir constantly until sauce reaches a boil, boil 1 minute then remove from heat. Sauce should heavily coat a spoon.

Mango Chutney

We developed this recipe to go with curries; then we discovered it was a great sandwich condiment. The chutney is also a quick appetizer when spooned over cream cheese and served with crackers.

Ingredients

4 cups fresh mango cubes

3/4 cup light brown sugar

1/2 cup light corn syrup

3/4 cup apple cider vinegar

2 limes, juice of

3/4 cup raisins

3/4 cup golden raisins

1/2 teaspoon dried minced onion

1 1/2 cloves garlic, minced

1 1/2 teaspoons kosher salt

1 1/2 teaspoons ground ginger

1/4 teaspoon ground cinnamon

1/4 teaspoon allspice

1/4 teaspoon cardamom

Pinch of cloves

Directions

Place all ingredients in a large stockpot. Heat to boiling then reduce heat and simmer 1 to 2 hours until a jam-like consistency.

While simmering chutney, sterilize 4 pint jars and lids by boiling in water for 10 minutes.

When the chutney has thickened, using a clean stainless steel ladle or serving spoon and a canning funnel, carefully spoon the hot chutney into the jars almost to the top making sure to keep the rims of the jars clean. If any chutney drips onto the jar rim, simply wipe it clean with a tea towel.

Once the jars are filled, screw the lids on tightly. While cooling, the jars will seal. There may be a pop sound indicating the jar has sealed. To test for seal, press the middle of the lid with a finger or thumb. If the lid springs up when you release your finger, the lid is unsealed. Store sealed jars in a cool dark place until ready to enjoy and unsealed jars in the refrigerator.

Orange Sauce

Ingredients

1/2 cup chicken broth

1/2 cup fresh squeezed orange juice with pulp

1 tablespoon white balsamic vinegar

1/4 cup orange marmalade, or more to taste

2 teaspoons grated orange zest

1 pinch cayenne pepper

1/2 teaspoon Chinese Five Spice

1 tablespoon arrowroot or cornstarch

2 tablespoons Grand Marnier

Directions

In a small saucepan over medium heat, whisk together chicken broth, orange juice, balsamic vinegar, orange marmalade, orange zest, cayenne pepper, Chinese Five Spice and arrowroot, bring to a boil for 1 minute. Stir in Grand Marnier.

Pour into a decorative pitcher.

Dark Sweet Cherry Sauce

Ingredients

1 tablespoon reserved duck fat or butter

1/4 cup finely chopped shallot

16 frozen dark sweet red cherries, thawed

1/2 cup chicken broth

2 tablespoons Sandeman Founder's Reserve Ruby Porto, port wine

1 tablespoon honey

1/2 teaspoon Herbes de Provence

1 1/2 tablespoons Minor's Demi Glace Sauce Concentrate

Directions

In a small saucepan over medium-low heat, add duck fat or butter and shallots; sauté 2 to 3 minutes until softened. Whisk in cherries, chicken broth, port wine, honey, and Herbes de Provence. Increase heat to medium and bring sauce to a gentle boil; stir in the Minor's Demi Glace Sauce Concentrate and heat until sauce thickens.

Pour into a decorative pitcher.

Bordelaise Red Wine Sauce

Ingredients

1 1/2 cups water

1/3 cup Minor's Beef Demi Glace Sauce Concentrate

1 1/2 cups Bordeaux or dry red wine

2 stems fresh thyme

1 bay leaf

1 shallot, sliced

2 cloves garlic, sliced

Freshly ground black pepper to taste

Directions

In large measuring cup, heat water to boiling in microwave oven, about 3 minutes; whisk in demi-glace sauce concentrate until smooth, set aside.

In a medium saucepan, add the wine, thyme, bay leaf, shallots, and garlic. Heat to boiling and reduce to simmer. Cook until the wine has reduced to about 1/3 cup. Strain and discard the herbs, shallot and garlic.

Return the wine to the saucepan, add the demi-glace and a grind of fresh pepper. Simmer on a medium low heat for 10-15 minutes.

Sauces from left to right: Champignon, Chasseur, and Bordelaise.

Champignon Sauce

Ingredients

1 tablespoon butter

2 tablespoons minced shallot

1 teaspoon minced garlic

3 tablespoons butter

8 ounces mushrooms, cleaned, trimmed, and sliced

1 cup beef broth

1/3 cup red wine

1 teaspoon Worcestershire sauce

1 bay leaf

1/4 teaspoon chopped fresh thyme

Kosher salt and freshly ground black pepper to taste

2 tablespoons Minor's Demi Glace Sauce Concentrate

Directions

Melt 1 tablespoon of butter in a saucepan over medium heat. Stir in shallot and garlic; cook until shallot has softened.

Add the 3 tablespoons of butter; once the butter has melted add the mushrooms. Cook and stir the mushrooms until they begin to soften, about 5 minutes.

Pour in the beef broth, red wine, and Worcestershire sauce; add bay leaf and thyme, and bring to a simmer over medium-high heat. Once simmering, season to taste with salt and pepper. Reduce the heat to medium-low; continue to cook, uncovered, until the sauce reduces slightly, about 30 minutes.

Stir in demi-glace, heat 1 minute. Remove the bay leaf before serving.

Chasseur Sauce

Chasseur is the French word for Hunter. This is another classic Escoffier recipe which complements beef, lamb, or game.

Ingredients

4 tablespoons butter, divided

2 large mushrooms, thinly sliced

1 tablespoon minced shallot

1 cup dry white wine

2 tablespoons VSOP Cognac

2 tablespoons tomato paste

1/4 cup prepared Minor's Demi Glace
(2 teaspoons in 1/4 cup water)

Freshly ground black pepper to taste

Kosher salt to taste

2 teaspoons finely chopped fresh chervil,
French parsley, or Italian parsley

Directions

Melt 1 tablespoon butter in a sauté pan over medium heat. Add the mushrooms to the pan and sauté until lightly browned. Add the shallots and sauté until translucent.

Deglaze the pan with white wine and Cognac; let it simmer until the alcohol has evaporated and the wine and Cognac is reduced by half.

Add the tomato paste and demi-glace. Bring to a simmer; simmer for 5 minutes and skim off any fat that floats to the surface.

Whisking constantly, add the remaining three tablespoons of butter one tablespoon at a time.

Season the sauce with pepper and salt to taste and whisk in the parsley.

Roasted Beef Tenderloin

Ingredients

1 center cut, 2 to 3 pounds, tenderloin of beef

3 tablespoons avocado oil

Kosher salt and freshly ground black pepper

Directions

Preheat oven to 425°F.

Bring beef to room temperature. Dry roast with paper towels. Brush with 1 tablespoon avocado oil and season tenderloin with salt and pepper.

Heat 2 tablespoons avocado oil until shimmering in a heavy skillet over medium high heat, place the tenderloin in the skillet and sear the tenderloin on each side. Place roast on a rack in shallow roasting pan.

Roast tenderloin as follows:

• 20 to 35 minutes for rare
• 35 to 40 minutes medium rare
• 40 to 45 minutes for medium
• 45 to 50 minutes for well-done

Remove roast when meat thermometer registers:

Medium-Rare - 125°F   Medium - 130°F
Medium-Well - 145°F   Well-Done - 150°F

Transfer roast to carving board; tent loosely with aluminum foil. Let the roast stand 10 to 15 minutes. Temperature will continue to rise about 10°F.

Roasted Tomato Crowns

Ingredients

1 tomato, washed and dry

1 clove garlic, minced

1/2 teaspoon fresh thyme leaves

1/8 teaspoon dry chili pepper flakes

1/8 teaspoon kosher salt

1/8 teaspoon freshly ground black pepper

1 tablespoon extra-virgin olive oil

1 tablespoon shredded Parmesan cheese

Directions

Preheat oven to 425°F.

Using a small sharp knife, in the outside center of the tomato start cutting a zig-zag pattern around the circumference of the tomato. Pull the two pieces apart, the halves will look like crowns.

In a small mixing bowl, mix together minced garlic, fresh thyme, chili pepper flakes, salt, pepper, and olive oil.

Place tomatoes on a parchment paper covered baking sheet, with a rim, flesh side up. Drizzle herb-olive oil over tomatoes and top with Parmesan cheese. Roast tomatoes in heated oven for 20 minutes.

Duchess Potatoes

To make ahead, prepare the mashed potatoes, pipe them and refrigerate.

Ingredients

1 1/2 pounds Russet of Yukon Gold potatoes, peeled, cut into chunks

1 teaspoon kosher salt

1 tablespoon heavy whipping cream

1 1/2 tablespoons butter

1/8 teaspoon nutmeg

1/8 teaspoon white pepper

2 egg yolks

1 tablespoon melted butter

Cayenne pepper

Directions

Preheat the oven to 425°F.

Place potatoes in a 3-quart saucepan and cover with a couple inches of cold water. Add salt to the water. Bring to a simmer and cook until the potatoes are fork tender, about 20 to 25 minutes; drain in a colander for 5 minutes.

Put the potatoes back in the saucepan and using a potato masher mash potatoes until smooth.

Add cream and butter and whisk the potatoes until smooth and creamy. Add the nutmeg, pepper, and salt to taste; then, whisk in the egg yolks.

Using a piping bag with a large open star tip, pipe 6 potato mounds onto a parchment paper covered cookie sheet. Gently brush the potatoes with the melted butter and sprinkle cayenne over the tops.

Bake for 20 minutes until potato ridges brown.

Béarnaise Sauce

Ingredients

1 1/2 tablespoons dry white wine

1 1/2 tablespoons white wine vinegar

1/4 teaspoon freshly ground black pepper

1 small shallot, peeled and finely minced

2 sprigs fresh tarragon

3 egg yolks, at room temperature

1/4 teaspoon kosher salt

16 tablespoons unsalted butter, cut into 1-inch cubes

1/2 tablespoon finely chopped tarragon leaves

1/2 tablespoon finely chopped Italian parsley

Directions

Place wine, vinegar, pepper, shallot and tarragon in a small saucepan over medium low heat. Simmer until reduced in half about 2 minutes, then remove from stove and let it stand for 5 minutes to infuse. Remove tarragon sprigs, cool 5 minutes before use.

Place egg yolks, infused vinegar, 8 tablespoons butter, and salt in small saucepan over lowest stovetop heat. Stir sauce continuously to incorporate butter into egg yolks. When butter is melted into yolks, add remaining 8 tablespoons butter and slowly melt butter into sauce. Stir sauce continuously until sauce has thickened.

Fold in finely chopped tarragon and parsley. To keep sauce warm, place sauce in a double boiler over warm water.

French Vanilla Ice Cream

Vanilla extract's primary function is to add flavor to the recipe but using 1 tablespoon of extract can contribute to a softer textured ice cream due to the alcohol content of the vanilla making it easier to scoop out of the container. Kathy uses her homemade vanilla extract for this recipe.

Ingredients

1 vanilla bean

1 1/4 cups granulated sugar

6 egg yolks

2 cups whole milk

2 cups heavy whipping cream

1 tablespoon vanilla extract

Directions

Using a paring knife, split open the vanilla bean and scrape out seeds. Put vanilla seeds into the sugar and mix to separate the vanilla seeds.

In a large saucepan, beat together the egg yolks and whole milk; beat in vanilla sugar, then add in the vanilla bean pod.

Cook ice cream batter over low heat, stirring constantly, until 165°F or slightly thickened. Mixture should smoothly coat a spoon. Remove from heat and strain, reserving vanilla bean. Cool, then add cream and vanilla and return vanilla bean to batter.

Refrigerate batter overnight. Freeze in ice cream machine per manufacturer's instruction.

Makes 1 quart.

Crème Fraîche

Crème Fraîche is a French soured cream. Homemade Crème Fraîche is so easy to make with only two ingredients and the result is creamy and tangy.

Ingredients

2 cups heavy whipping cream

3 tablespoons cultured buttermilk

Directions

Combine cream and buttermilk in a glass jar. Cover tightly with cheesecloth (or any breathable material) and let sit at room temperature (70 to 75 degrees F or 21 to 24 degrees C) until thickened, about 24 hours.

Stir mixture, then screw on the lid. Refrigerate for 24 hours before using.

Heavy Simple Syrup

Ingredients

1/4 cup water

1/2 cup granulated sugar

Directions

Prepare simple syrup by bringing water to a boil in a saucepan, stirring in sugar and boiling just until sugar is dissolved.

Orange Sherbet

There is no substitute for freshly squeezed orange juice with the pulp in this recipe. The flavors of this sherbet are reminiscent of an orange creamsicle.

Ingredients

1 1/2 cups freshly squeezed orange juice with pulp

3/4 cup ultrafine granulated sugar

1/2 cup heavy whipping cream

3/4 cup whole milk

1 tablespoon orange zest

1/8 teaspoon kosher salt

2 tablespoons Grand Marnier

Directions

In a small saucepan, bring 1/2 cup orange juice and sugar to a boil then reduce to a simmer for 10 minutes, remove from heat and stir in the remaining orange juice. Whisk together cream, whole milk, orange zest and Grand Marnier and whisk into the orange juice.

Freeze in ice cream maker according to manufacturer's instructions.

Crêpes

Ingredients

2 eggs

1 cup all-purpose flour

1 cup milk

1 tablespoon granulated sugar

Finely grated zest of 1/2 orange and 1/2 lemon

4 tablespoons butter, melted

2 tablespoons Grand Marnier

4 tablespoons clarified butter

Directions

In a medium bowl, whisk together the eggs and milk then whisk in flour, sugar, orange and lemon zests until smooth; the batter will be thick. Whisk in the melted butter and Grand Marnier. Let batter rest 30 minutes.

Heat a teaspoon of clarified butter in an 8-inch skillet or crêpe pan. Ladle or pour in enough batter and tilt the skillet around to cover the bottom of the skillet evenly.

Cook the crêpe until bubbles form on the surface and the edges turn light brown. Loosen edges of crêpe and turn crêpe over. Cook the crêpe a few seconds until the second side is a light brown. Slide the crêpe out of skillet.

For the extra crêpes, separate the crêpes with parchment paper, wrap tightly with plastic wrap and freeze.

About 12 6-inch crêpes.

Chocolate Ganache Sauce

Ingredients

6 ounces Ghirardelli or Guittard 60% Cacao Bittersweet Chocolate, chopped in small pieces

1 tablespoon butter

1/2 cup heavy whipping cream

4 tablespoons ultrafine sugar

2 tablespoons liqueur or pear brandy

Directions

Place chocolate and butter in small bowl

In a saucepan bring heavy cream and sugar to a boil. Pour boiling cream over chopped chocolate and butter. Whisk until smooth and chocolate is melted.

Stir in liqueur or pear brandy for Crêpes D' Anjou.

About 1 1/2 cups sauce.

Banana Ice Cream

Ingredients

6 ounces granulated sugar

1/2 vanilla bean

1 1/2 cups whole milk

5 egg yolks

1 1/2 cups heavy whipping cream

3 ounces pureed banana

1 tablespoon 99 Bananas Liqueur

Directions

Place sugar in bowl. Split vanilla bean pod and using a sharp paring knife scrape the seeds out of the pod and place into the bowl of sugar; mix vanilla seeds into the sugar to separate the seeds.

Place milk and sugar in 3-quart saucepan, stir to mix. Beat in egg yolks and put vanilla bean in saucepan. Over medium heat, bring mixture to 165°F then remove from heat. Strain mixture, place vanilla bean back in ice cream batter.

Mix together cream, pureed banana, and 99 Bananas Liqueur; add cream mixture to the milk. Cool ice cream batter in refrigerator overnight. Transfer mixture to an ice cream maker and freeze following the manufacturer's instructions. Reserve ice cream in freezer until ready to assemble the dessert.

For Baked Alaska, freeze the frozen banana ice cream in a semi sphere cocoa bomb mold.

French Walnut
Sponge Cake

Ingredients

4 ounces egg yolks

3 ounces granulated sugar

4 ounces egg whites

3 ounces sifted all-purpose flour

2 1/2 ounces finely chopped walnuts

Directions

Preheat oven to 400°F.

Butter 7" x 11" bake pan, line bottom with parchment paper, and butter paper.

In a small mixer bowl, beat egg yolks with 1 ounce sugar until very thick, lemon colored, and yolks fall in a ribbon from whip, about 5 minutes.

In a large mixer bowl, beat egg whites with remaining 2 ounces of sugar until stiff with medium peaks. Gradually fold egg yolk mixture into egg whites. Sift flour, in thirds, over egg mixture and gently fold in the flour. Sprinkle with chopped walnuts and fold walnuts into the batter.

Spread batter into parchment lined bake pan. Bake 12 minutes until toothpick comes out clean. When cooled completely, remove parchment paper and cut into 3-inch rounds and set aside.

Apricot Compote

Ingredients

1 bag (6 ounces) dried apricots

1 tablespoon granulated sugar

1 star anise

1 whole clove

1/2 vanilla pod split lengthwise

3/4 cup freshly squeezed orange juice with pulp

3/4 cup water

Zest of 1 orange

2 tablespoons Cointreau

Directions

Cut each apricot in thirds lengthwise and in fourths widthwise for 12 pieces for each apricot.

Put all compote ingredients, except Cointreau, into heavy bottom pan, bring mixture to boil. Reduce heat and simmer until apricots absorb most of the liquid, about 45 to 60 minutes, with remaining liquid forming a syrup.

Remove from heat and pour in Cointreau, chill compote.

Swiss Meringue

Ingredients

8 large egg whites, at room temperature

2 cups granulated sugar

1/4 teaspoon cream of tartar

1 teaspoon pure vanilla extract

Directions

Fill medium saucepan one quarter full with water. Set the saucepan over medium heat and bring water to a simmer.

Combine egg whites, sugar, and cream of tartar in the heatproof bowl of an electric mixer and place over saucepan. Whisk egg whites and sugar constantly until sugar is dissolved and whites are warm to the touch and no granular feel when rubbing between fingers.

Transfer bowl to electric mixer fitted with the whisk attachment. Whip, starting on low and increasing speed to high, until stiff, glossy peaks form, about 10 minutes. Mix in vanilla. Use meringue immediately.

Whipped Cream

Powdered sugar, also known as confectioners' sugar, can help stabilize whipped cream and make it last longer.

Powdered sugar has cornstarch which helps whipped cream keep its shape and be fluffier, and it can last up to 12 hours in the refrigerator.

Ingredients

1/2 cup cold heavy whipping cream

1 tablespoon powdered sugar

1/2 teaspoon pure vanilla extract

Directions

Place a medium-sized bowl (preferably metal) and mixer beaters in the freezer to chill. Once the bowl and beaters have chilled, remove from freezer and add heavy cream, powdered sugar, and vanilla extract to the bowl.

Using a handheld electric mixer, beat ingredients on low speed, gradually increasing speed to high, and beat until stiff peaks form, about 3 to 4 minutes.

Use immediately or cover tightly and chill in the refrigerator for up to 12 hours.

About 1 cup whipped cream.

The Finale Act

This last story is about when Darrell and I left the Rodeway Inn to finish high school. I was talking to one of my fellow former workers and he shared this story with me, and my wife insisted that I share this story with you because she found it to be humorous.

While Darrell and I were working at the Rodeway Inn and, unbeknownst to us, our coworkers developed a nickname for us besides "The Twins". We were also known as "Flame On 1" and "Flame On 2" being in reference to our being Flambé Chefs. Now, what made the names interesting is when we left, they started calling our predecessors Scorch 1 and Scorch 2, wasn't it Shakespeare who said, "What is in a name." apparently had not heard of our predecessors!

In the final act of being a Flambé Chef, Darrell and I resigned from being employees of the restaurant industry to concentrate on graduating from high school. My twin then went into the Air Force upon completing high school and I went on to graduate from my local college. We both remained in the Food Service Industry, with my twin becoming a Bar Manager and I became a Manufacturer's Representative for Hollymatic, the people who invented the hamburger patty machine.

INDEX

A

Apples
   Bourbon Whiskey Apple Flambé.........................112
   Kathy's Apple & Banana Flambé.........................120
   Pork Medallions with Apples & Calvados.............91
Apricots
   Apricot Compote..188
   Pears with Rum Apricot Sauce..............................134
   Pork Chops with Flaming Apricot Bourbon Sauce
  94

B

Bacon
   Scallops with Peach Chutney Bourbon Sauce.......33
   Wilted Spinach Salad..22
Banana Liqueur 99 Banana
   Banana Ice Cream...184
   Brennan's Inspired Bananas Foster....................113
   Caribbean Bananas Flambé..................................116
Bananas
   Banana Ice Cream...184
   Brennan's Inspired Bananas Foster....................113
   Caribbean Bananas Flambé..................................116
   Jamaican Bananas Flambé.....................................117
   Kathy's Apple & Banana Flambé.........................120
   Plantation Surprise..131
Beef
   Châteaubriand Bouquétiere....................................80
   Roasted Beef Tenderloin.......................................172
   Delmonico's Inspired Steak Diane........................74
   Steak Au Poivre..81
   Steak Diane..71
   Steak Tartare..27
   Tournedos of Beef...77
   Veal Chops with Cognac Cream Sauce.................85
   Veal Scallops with Cognac Mushroom Sauce.......84
Bourbon Whiskey
   Bourbon Peach Flambé...108
   Bourbon Whiskey Apple Flambé.........................112
   Flaming Prawns Diablo...49
   Flaming Prawns in a Bourbon Tomato Cream
   Sauce..46
   Pork Chops with Flaming Apricot Bourbon Sauce
  94
   Scallops with Peach Chutney Bourbon Sauce.......33

C

Cake
   French Walnut Sponge Cake................................187
Calvados Apple Brandy
   Kathy's Apple & Banana Flambé.........................120
   Pork Medallions with Apples & Calvados.............91
Caramel
   Café Royale...154
Châteaubriand Bouquétiere..80
Cheeses
   Brie
      Cranberries & Sizzling Brie...........................29
   Goat
      Stuffed Chicken Breasts with Mango Chutney
      Sauce..62
   Parmesan
      Caeser Salad...23
      Scallops Flambé...52
Cherries
   Cherries Jubilee..126
   Dark Sweet Cherry Sauce....................................168
   Flamed Duck Breasts à l'Dark Sweet Cherry Sauce
  69
   Lamb Chops with Cognac & Cherry Demi-Glace
  95
   Lollipop Lamb Chops with Cherry Sauce.......25, 99
   Pork Medallions with Cherry Infused Sauce.......87
Chicken
   Brandied Chicken..63
   Chicken Livers Supreme...68
   Stuffed Chicken Breasts with Mango Chutney
   Sauce..62
Chocolate
   Chocolate Ganache Sauce....................................183
   Crêpes D'Anjou...138
Coffee
   Café Brûlot Diabolique..151
   Café Royale...154

Irish Coffee............148
Spanish Coffee............145
Cognac
Between The Sheets Flambé............127
Brandied Chicken............63
Café Brûlot Diabolique............151
Café Royale............154
Châteaubriand Bouquétiere............80
Crab Legs Voltaire............53
Crab Legs Voltaire II............58
Delmonico's Inspired Steak Diane............74
Flamed Duck Breasts à l'Dark Sweet Cherry Sauce
............69
Flamed Duck Breasts à l'Orange Sauce............69
Flamed Lamb Chops............97
Lamb Chops with Cognac & Cherry Demi-Glace
............95
Lobster Thermidor............59
Meatballs of Fire!............32
Ragin' Cajun Prawns............43
Scallops Flambé............52
Steak Au Poivre............81
Steak Diane............71
Stuffed Chicken Breasts with Mango Chutney
Sauce............62
Tournedos of Beef............77
Veal Chops with Cognac Cream Sauce............85
Veal Scallops with Cognac Mushroom Sauce......84
Wilted Spinach Salad............167
Créme Fraîche............179
Croutons
Caeser Croutons............159

D
Desserts
Between The Sheets Flambé............127
Bourbon Peach Flambé............108
Bourbon Whiskey Apple Flambé............112
Brennan's Inspired Bananas Foster............113
Caribbean Bananas Flambé............116
Cherries Jubilee............126
Crêpes Suzette............121
Crêpes D'Anjou............138
Flaming Baked Alaska's............141
Jamaican Bananas Flambé............117
Kathy's Apple & Banana Flambé............120
Mango Flambé............130

Peaches Flambé............106
Pear Flambé............135
Pears with Rum Apricot Sauce............134
Plantation Surprise............131
Strawberries Romanoff............109
Duck Breast
Flamed Duck Breasts à l'Dark Sweet Cherry Sauce
............69
Flamed Duck Breasts à l'Orange Sauce............69

F
Flaming Baked Alaska's
Apricot Compote............188
Banana Ice Cream............184
Swiss Meringue............189
French Walnut Sponge Cake............187
Frangelico Liqueur
Pears with Rum Apricot Sauce............134

G
Grand Marnier
Café Brûlot Diabolique............151
Cranberries & Sizzling Brie............29
Crêpes Suzette............121
Kathy's Apple & Banana Flambé............120
Mango Flambé............130
Peaches Flambé............106
Plantation Surprise............131
Strawberries Romanoff............109

H
Heavy Simple Syrup............180

I
Ice Creams & Sherbet
Banana Ice Cream............184
French Vanilla Ice Cream............176
Between the Sheets Flambé............127
Bourbon Peach Flambé............108
Bourbon Whiskey Apple Flambé............112
Brennan's Inspired Bananas Foster............113
Caribbean Bananas Flambé............116
Cherries Jubilee............126
Flaming Baked Alaska's............141
Jamaican Bananas Flambé............117
Kathy's Apple & Banana Flambé............120
Mango Flambé............130

196

Peaches Flambé..106

Pear Flambé..135

Pears with Rum Apricot Sauce.........................134

Orange Sherbet...181

Plantation Surprise..131

K

Kahlua

  Spanish Coffee..145

Kirschwasser

  Cherries Jubilee..126

  Lollipop Lamb Chops with Cherry Sauce.......25, 99

  Pork Medallions with Cherry Infused Sauce 87

L

Lamb

  Flamed Lamb Chops..97

  Lamb Chops with Cognac & Cherry Demi-Glace

 95

  Lollipop Lamb Chops with Cherry Sauce.......25, 99

  Meatballs of Fire!...32

Lobster

  Lobster Thermidor..59

  Lobster Thermidor Sauce...............................165

  Thermidor Lobster Stock................................163

  Thermidor Mushrooms...................................164

M

Mango

  Stuffed Chicken Breasts with Mango Chutney

  Sauce..62

  Mango Chutney..166

  Mango Flambé...130

  Plantation Surprise.......................................131

Meringue

  Swiss Meringue...189

Mushrooms

  Chanterelles

    Brandied Chicken..63

  Cremini

    Delmonico's Inspired Steak Diane.....................74

    Scallops Flambé..52

    Crab Legs Voltaire...53

    Crab Legs Voltaire II......................................58

    Lobster Thermidor...59

    Steak Diane..71

    Thermidor Mushrooms...................................164

Veal Chops with Cognac Cream Sauce...............85

N

Nuts

  Cashews

    Jamaican Bananas Flambé..............................117

  Hazelnuts

    Pears with Rum Apricot Sauce.........................134

  Macadamia

    Brennan's Inspired Bananas Foster...................113

    Plantation Surprise.......................................131

  Pecans

    Caribbean Bananas Flambé.............................116

    Flaming Prawns Diablo...................................49

    Sweet & Spicy Candied Pecans........................162

    Flaming Prawns in a Bourbon Tomato Cream

    Sauce...46

  Walnuts

    French Walnut Sponge Cake............................187

O

Old Bushmills Black Bush Irish Whiskey

  Irish Coffee..148

  Spanish Coffee..145

Orange Sauce...167

P

Peaches

  Bourbon Peach Flambé....................................108

  Peach Chutney...161

  Scallops with Peach Chutney Bourbon Sauce.......33

  Peaches Flambé..106

Pears

  Crêpes D'Anjou..138

  Pear Flambé..135

  Pears with Rum Apricot Sauce.........................134

Pineapple

  Between the Sheets Flambé..............................127

  Plantation Surprise.......................................131

Pork

  Meatballs of Fire!...32

  Pork Chops with Flaming Apricot Bourbon Sauce

 94

  Pork Medallions with Apples & Calvados............91

  Pork Medallions with Cherry Infused Sauce.......87

Port Wine

  Pork Medallions with Cherry Infused Sauce.......87

Potatoes

Duchess Potatoes.................................174
Prawns
   Flaming Prawns Diablo.............................49
   Flaming Prawns in a Bourbon Tomato Cream
     Sauce..46
   Prawns Gargantua..............................42
   Ragin' Cajun Prawns...........................43

R

Red Wine
   Bordelaise Red Wine Sauce....................169
   Champignon Sauce.............................170
   Flamed Lamb Chops............................97
Rum
  Bacardi White
   Kathy's Apple & Banana Flambé...............120
   Pears with Rum Apricot Sauce................134
  Don Q 151
   Brennan's Inspired Bananas Foster.............113
   Cranberries & Sizzling Brie....................29
   Cherries Jubilee.............................126
   Crêpes Suzette..............................121
   Peaches Flambé.............................106
   Pear Flambé.................................135
   Plantation Surprise..........................131
  Malibu
   Caribbean Bananas Flambé...................116
   Between The Sheets Flambé...................127
  Meyers's Dark
   Between the Sheets Flambé...................127
   Caribbean Bananas Flambé...................116
   Jamaican Bananas Flambé....................117
   Mango Flambé..............................130

S

Salads
   Caesar Salad.................................23
   Wilted Spinach Salad.........................22
Sauces
   Béarnaise Sauce.............................175
   Bordelaise Red Wine Sauce...................169
   Chasseur Sauce.............................171
   Champignon Sauce..........................170
   Chocolate Ganache Sauce....................183
   Crème Fraîche..............................179
   Dark Sweet Cherry Sauce....................168
   Orange Sauce...............................167

Peach Chutney................................161
Yogurt Sauce................................160
Scallops
   Scallops Flambé..............................52
   Scallops with Peach Chutney Bourbon Sauce......33
Seafood
  Anchovies
   Caeser Salad.................................23
  Dungeness Crab
   Crab Legs Voltaire............................53
   Crab Legs Voltaire II..........................58
  Lobster
   Lobster Thermidor............................59
  Prawns
   Flaming Prawns Diablo.......................49
   Flaming Prawns in a Bourbon Tomato Cream
     Sauce......................................46
   Prawns Gargantua............................42
   Ragin' Cajun Prawns..........................43
  Scallops
   Scallops Flambé..............................52
   Scallops with Peach Chutney Bourbon Sauce.....33
Sherry
   Chicken Livers Supreme........................68
   Crab Legs Voltaire............................53
   Crab Legs Voltaire II..........................58
   Prawns Gargantua............................42
   Steak Tartare.................................27
Spinach
   Wilted Spinach Salad.........................22
Strawberries
   Strawberries Romanoff......................109
Simple Syrup
   Crêpes Suzette..............................121
   Heavy Simple Syrup.........................180
   Plantation Surprise..........................131
Starters
   Caeser Salad.................................23
   Cranberries & Sizzling Brie....................29
   Lollipop Lamb Chops with Cherry Sauce...........25
   Meatballs of Fire!............................32
   Scallops with Peach Chutney Bourbon Sauce......33
   Steak Tartare.................................27
   Wilted Spinach Salad........................167

T

Tia Maria

Spanish Coffee...145
Triple Sec Liqueur
  Peaches Flambé..106
Tomatoes
  Roasted Tomato Crowns....................................173

V
Veal
  Veal Chops with Cognac Cream Sauce.................85
  Veal Scallops with Cognac Mushroom Sauce......84
Vegetables
  Duchess Potatoes...174
  Roasted Tomato Crowns..................................173

W
Williams Pear Brandy
  Crêpes D'Anjou..138
Whipped Cream
  Whipped Cream..190
  Café Brûlot Diabolique...................................151
  Café Royale..154
  Irish Coffee...148
  Spanish Coffee..145
  Strawberries Romanoff....................................109

Y
Yogurt Sauce
  Meatballs of Fire!..32

www.ingramcontent.com/pod-product-compliance
Lightning Source LLC
Chambersburg PA
CBHW041113120626
46547CB00019B/2696